1978

1978

PEOPLES OF THE EARTH

volume twelve
Indian Subcontinent
(Including Ceylon)
THE DANBURY PRESS

(Preceding page)
One small part of the endless
cycle reaches its close as
male friends and relatives
carry a body to its funeral
pyre. The span of one
lifetime is like a bead on a
necklace. Behind stretch
past lives and in the future,
lives yet to be. Each soul
or *atman* strives through
successive rebirths to
win liberation from worldly
sorrow and achieve union
with the one — with Brahman.

Contents

Supervisory Editor of the Series:
Professor Sir Edward Evans-Pritchard,
Fellow of All Souls, Professor of Social Anthropology,
University of Oxford, 1946-1970,
Chevalier de la Légion d'Honneur

Volume Editor:
Christoph von Fürer-Haimendorf,
Professor of Asian Anthropology in the
University of London, author of *Morals and Merit* etc

The DANBURY PRESS
a division of GROLIER ENTERPRISES INC.

Publisher
ROBERT B. CLARKE

© 1973 Europa Verlag

Library of Congress Catalog Card No. 72 85614

Printed in Italy by
Arnoldo Mondadori Editore, Verona

Editorial Director **Tom Stacey**

Picture Director **Alexander Low**
Executive Editor **Katherine Ivens**
Art Director **Tom Deas**
Assistant Editor **Elisabeth Meakin**
Project Co-ordinator **Anne Harrison**
Research **Cheryl Moyer**

Specialist Picture Research **Elly Beintema**
Picture Research **Claire Baines**
Diana Eggitt
Jeanne Griffiths
Carolyn Keay
Emma Stacey

Editorial Assistants **Richard Carlisle**
Rosamund Ellis
J M Marrin
Susan Rutherford
Pamela Tubby
Editorial Secretary **Caroline Silverman**
Design Assistant **Susan Forster**
Richard Kelly
Cartography **Ron Haywood**
Illustrations **Sandra Archibald, Ron McTrusty**

Production **Roger Multon**
Production Editor **Vanessa Charles**

The publishers gratefully acknowledge help from
the following organizations:
Royal Anthropological Institute, London
Musée de l'Homme, Paris
International African Institute, London
British Museum, London
Royal Geographical Society, London
Scott Polar Research Institute, Cambridge
Royal Asiatic Society, London
Royal Central Asian Society, London
Pitt-Rivers Museum, Oxford
Horniman Museum, London
Institute of Latin American Studies, London

Photographic Credits

Cover – **Bruno Barbey** (Magnum from the John Hillelson Agency),
Brian Brake (The John Hillelson Agency), **Ken Heyman, Alexander
Low, Roland Michaud** (Rapho, Paris), **Marilyn Silverstone** (Magnum
from the John Hillelson Agency), **Raghubir Singh** (The John Hillelson
Agency). 114 through 123, 125 through 127 – **Bruno Barbey** (Magnum
from the John Hillelson Agency). 58 through 60, 62 through 65, 68
through 71 – **Brian Brake** (The John Hillelson Agency). 74 – **F.P.G.**
108 – **C. von Fürer-Haimendorf.** 56, 57 – **Ross Greetham.** 128, 129 –
Haddon Photographic Collection (Cambridge University). 48, 49 (top
lt.) – **Ken Heyman.** 107 – **William Hubbell** (F.P.G.). 2, 3, 44 through 47,
61 – **Alexander Low.** 124 – **Sylvia Matheson** (Robert Harding Associates).
110 through 113 – **Roland Michaud** (Rapho, Paris). 109 – **T. S. Satyan**
(Black Star, New York). 49 (bot. lt.), 95, 97 (center lt.), 98 through
105 – **Marilyn Silverstone** (Magnum from the John Hillelson Agency).
10-11, 16, 17, 19 through 43, 76 through 93, 97 (top lt.) – **Raghubir
Singh** (The John Hillelson Agency). 54, 55 – **Stella Snead.** 72, 73
– **Syndication International.** 50 through 52 – **Bruce Tapper.**

Peoples of the Earth, volumes one to twenty

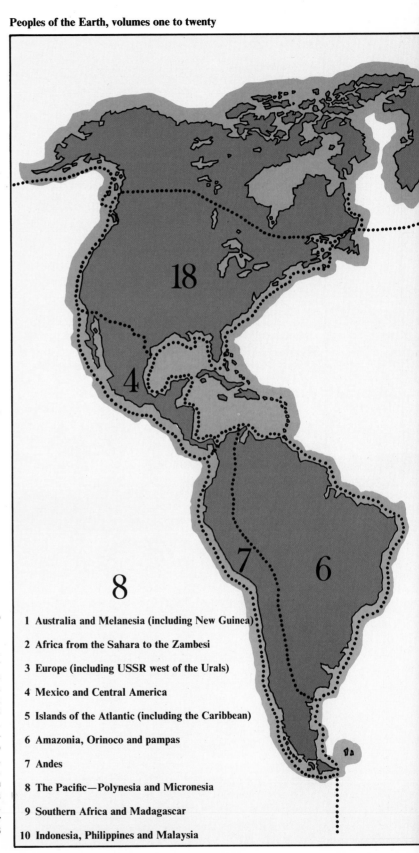

1 **Australia and Melanesia (including New Guinea)**

2 **Africa from the Sahara to the Zambesi**

3 **Europe (including USSR west of the Urals)**

4 **Mexico and Central America**

5 **Islands of the Atlantic (including the Caribbean)**

6 **Amazonia, Orinoco and pampas**

7 **Andes**

8 **The Pacific—Polynesia and Micronesia**

9 **Southern Africa and Madagascar**

10 **Indonesia, Philippines and Malaysia**

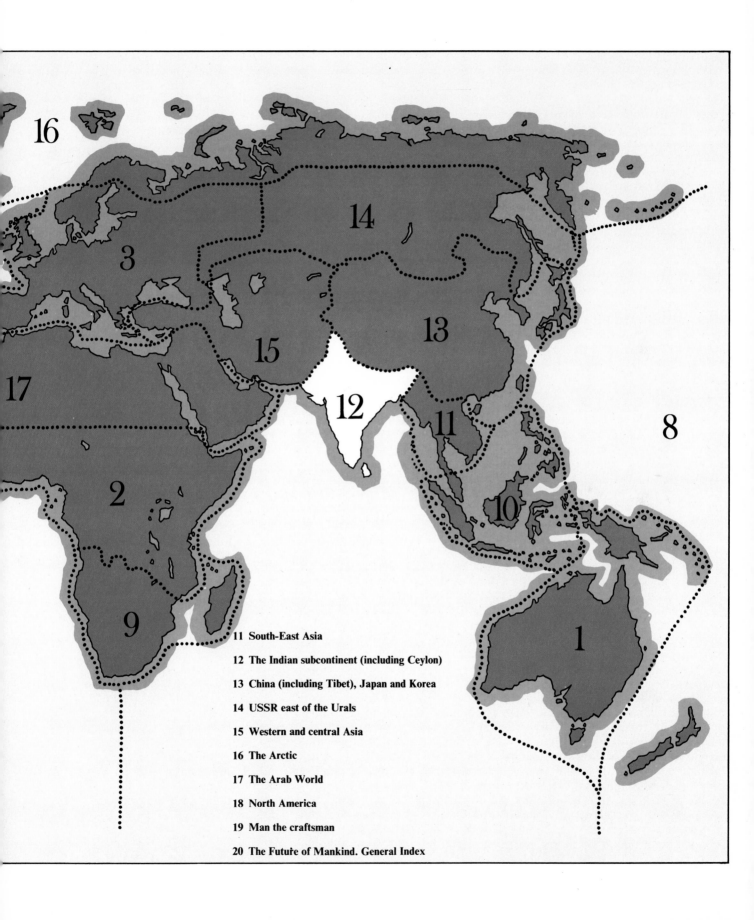

Social Stratification

Foreigners are fascinated with the caste system for two reasons. First it appears to exist all over India, cutting across the linguistic, regional and even religious boundaries between Indian communities. Second, it seems to rank social groups by birth absolutely. One group is superior or inferior to another in status and prestige, wealth and power. Compared with other forms of social stratification, like those based on social classes, estates, or a political party (as in the Soviet Union), the Indian caste system strikes foreigners as peculiarly rigid – and a system that is like nothing else outside India.

The true nature of this peculiarly Indian form of social stratification lies between these extreme positions: Indian society is not immobile nor is it in all its aspects unique.

Inequalities of status and prestige, power and wealth between groups of people exist elsewhere in the world as they do in India. In the industrial nations how much wealth or power you possess tends to determine your status and prestige. For the industrial nations it is a system of achieved statuses, where mobility 'from rags to riches' is meant to be quite commonplace and where the pattern of social stratification is not supposed to be bounded by a system of statuses that are ascribed permanently by birth – either directly (as in the case of an aristocracy), or indirectly (by providing superior education and other opportunities). Birth does of course continue to direct the mobility of individuals and groups; and in these societies there are further barriers of birth such as race and nationality. No black man has yet become President of the USA and in Britain Irish and Welsh nationalists continue to voice dissatisfaction with what they regard as a discriminatory economic structure.

Industry and cities in India began to grow on a wide scale with the consolidation of British rule. It led to over-population and extremely uneven regional development. Only since India's independence in 1947 have the speed and direction of industrial development been controlled and channeled for the welfare of the Indian people as a whole. Social stratification in today's India is marked by continuity as well as by change. Most Indians continue to live as village farmers.

'Caste' does not feature as a word in any of the indigenous Indian languages. It is derived from the Portuguese word 'castas', which Portuguese traders used to describe the closed groups of Indians they met on the Indian west coast in the 18th century. The word has become widely accepted as a translation of the Hindu word *jati* which means 'species', and its equivalents in other Indian languages. In a local caste system each *jati* occupies a rank above or below other *jati*. With each rank go certain typical customs. The people who live by this system are aware that a certain kind of behavior, especially pertaining to eating and marrying within the group, is expected of a caste. The minutiae of all these interactions within and between castes, which to outside observers seem so complex, are to Indians a pattern of life. In the small-scale society which Indian villagers, especially, inhabit this provides an easy means of identification.

Throughout India the castes are divided into *varna*, or ritual categories, a scheme which Indians find convenient for establishing the social identities of individuals and groups all over the country. Literally translated *varna* means 'color', but it actually refers to the classical division of Hindu society into four classes, the Brahman (priest), the Kshatriya (warrior), the Vaishya (merchant) and the Shudra (servant). Most Indian castes can be roughly divided into these four classes. The classes which stand outside the *varna* scheme are known as untouchables. The lowest ranking groups of the Hindus are called outcastes as they are formed from groups of people who for some reason have been excommunicated from their own caste. Even the non-Hindus of India – Muslims, Christians, Sikhs, Jains, Parsees, and Jews – are divided into groups resembling castes. These too are assigned a place within the *varna* scheme or, as more often occurs, outside it.

The caste system is rigid in the sense that once a person is born into a caste he cannot normally change it. The castes of the Brahman *varna* are the highest in rank and status, whereas the castes of the Shudra *varna* are lowest, while castes of the two middle classes come in between. The castes practise endogamy, which means that the members of a caste arrange marriages within their own caste. In practice the unit outside which the member of a caste may not marry is an even smaller subdivision of his caste, known among scholars as 'subcaste', but called by the people themselves their *jati* – the same word that they use for the larger group. Although the educated people in cosmopolitan cities ignore subcaste restrictions on their marriages, most marriages in modern India are still arranged by parents, strictly within the caste or subcaste.

Although the caste system has a restrictive influence on Indian economic development in practice, there has always been leeway for *jati* to change their occupation, contrary to the way the classical *varna* scheme fixed Hindus' occupations by birth. The colonial period of India's recent past tended on the whole to discourage the breaking-up of small-scale communities of farmers. In the name of non-interference with certain traditions and the hallowed practices of the subject people, there was little government planning for economic development and this gave privileged groups in the countryside unprecedented opportunities to get the best jobs in industry, trade and politics. Legislation did sometimes give the Shudra and untouchable castes the chance to improve their economic position and the constraints of the *varna* scheme did not then prevent them from branching out into non-traditional and lucrative occupations. Yet changes resulting from this status mobility were very limited. The lower castes simply imitated high caste practices because these seemed to be the most highly desirable, and indeed represented the only possible value that could be attained under conditions of dependent political status. There was more flexibility of occupations. As early as the beginning of the 20th century it was common to find a Brahman doctor or an office clerk who belonged to the goldsmith caste.

In several areas of India the *jajmani* system, by which occupationally specialized castes and agriculturists exchange goods and services, is breaking down. This tendency is more marked in poor or constantly unproductive farming areas. Paradoxically it destroys the customary security of the poorer sections of the community without creating alternative security for them. In areas where the 'green revolution' has been successful the customary links between the rural economy and the caste-class system remain unimpaired.

Because social stratification and political activity are linked in so many both traditional and modern ways Indian society shows both change and continuity. In many villages of India there are – at the subcaste level – councils of elders, known as *panchayat*, who keep law and order within their groups and often send representatives to caste associations based in a city or a town. Since discrimination on the basis of caste is illegal under the Indian constitution matters such as marriage outside the subcaste cannot be taken up and judged by the government law and order machinery. Such subjects are tackled by the caste *panchayat* at the village level and by caste associations in towns.

Caste associations existed during the 18th and 19th centuries in different regions of India including those native states of central India which never came under the full jurisdiction of British rule. Decisions of the caste councils and associations were subject to approval and arbitration by the ruler both in the areas fully administered by the British and, more especially, in partly autonomous states. Matters affecting caste lay within the royal court's arbitration, and rulers are known to have promoted or demoted whole castes in the local and regional ranking system. But the *varna* of a caste was not drastically altered. The rulers' interference could enhance or decrease a caste's status and prestige only within fairly narrow limits. British rule, on the other hand, seems to have combined with the policy of avoiding direct interference the creation of a legal super-structure which closely followed the interpretation of Hindu custom furnished by specially employed Brahman literati. The caste associations, especially of the Brahman castes, took a new lease of life from this operation. Indeed they became the recruiting ground of caste-based political parties in urban areas. The higher and middle non-Brahman castes, who were also receiving a restricted western education biased towards a role of service to society, accordingly extended their caste association activities to take in social reform and setting up political parties.

For the first ten years after India's independence these caste associations that grew up just before independence seem to have channeled much of the country's democratic politics along caste lines. In the context of these political activities the castes changed their identity. They were neither the small local *jati* (castes or subcastes) nor the universal classical Indian *varna*. These caste associations, although still known by *jati* names, were based on their traditional appeal to a largely migrant urban population from many localities. Except where a political party based on a caste association could forge strong links with villagers and capture government power (as did the DMK in the southern state of Tamilnad), the political role of caste associations has been as ephemeral, and changes as rapidly, as the composition of central and state legislatures from one election to the next. And outside the restricted sphere of family disputes, marriage regulation, and the general preservation of a cultural heritage the caste *panchayat* and associations have largely ceased to play an important role. With the growing political maturity of the Indian electorate a new political party is increasingly unlikely to grow around a caste nucleus.

In rural areas, where the caste system imperceptibly merges into a social class system, it depends very much on the rural political processes in a given area whether the social class system develops into a system of antagonistic classes which reconstructs the caste system's hierarchy of ascribed status. In theory Indians should be able to create a more enlightened division of labor system than the old closed system in which wealth and power are distributed simply by the chance of birth, while continuing to live by their cultural heritage of caste. In this cultural heritage ritual and ceremony are important elements. These merge on the one hand with habitual moral discipline, and on the other with religion. This lies at the heart of the connection between Hinduism as an accepted way of life in India and *jati* as an ideological system. In this sense the issue of caste is separate from the issue of a more rational productive division of labor. And it has to be considered separately from this distribution of power in society.

There is much evidence that caste values coexist with the kind of economic activity called for by urban industry. Here lie the clues to the future pattern of social stratification in the country. In the textile mills of Bombay and Poona and in the steel mills of Jamshedpur in Bihar labor is recruited and jobs are allocated without regard for the workers' caste. Unfortunately studies of these situations reveal little about the workers' behavior while not at work. Nevertheless there is enough information to suggest that where houses are allocated by the factory management, the pressures of need and availability over-ride any scruples of caste that the workers might have even against living alongside untouchables and outcastes. The same is true in public places. When eating out or traveling by buses and trains the minutiae of proper inter-caste behavior are as easy to ignore as they are to observe at home. The lives of Jat villagers in Delhi state are divided between a village home and an urban place of work. As 'urban villagers' they are able to adapt their behavior according to the demands of their social setting without any traces of schizophrenia. This easy adjustment of behavior between home and the shop-floor among caste Hindus working in factories in western and eastern India, between village and city among the Jats of north India and between home and office among the successful Tamil Brahman businessmen and professionals, is not confined to a single area nor to castes at a certain level of the traditional hierarchy.

It seems that sometimes when farmers join city life, technological change is accompanied by organized exploitation without social change. At other times there is disorganized conflict and social upheaval. Whichever happens the pattern of social stratification in India detaches itself more and more from the cultural heritage of caste.

There are Indian settlers in many parts of the world, not only in the former British colonies of Africa and Asia, but also in Britain and Canada, who work as farmers, wage-laborers, businessmen and professionals. Studies of these overseas Indian communities also highlight the Indian caste system's adaptability and its capacity to coexist with other forms of social stratification. These communities have arrived at different times and in different ways. Some of the communities form much larger proportions of the total host population. Some live in the town, some in the country. Some have much closer links with India than others.

The social and economic situations of their derivation are so diverse and they originate from many different parts of India, yet they share a common cultural heritage of caste which, in these alien settings, has but a minimal economic and political role. Irrespective of their positions in caste hierarchy overseas Indians have entered the strata of wealth and power that exist in their host societies. It is interesting that while the potentially divisive functions of the indigenous caste system have fallen by the wayside, the cohesive ritual and cultural functions (like those of endogamy and ceremonial observances) have tended to be preserved though in a modified form. Weddings and other ceremonies that mark the life cycle require the services of a member of the priestly caste, of the drummer caste and perhaps also of one born into a caste of barbers. A miniature division of labor based on caste lines is preserved to fulfill these. But the very same priests, barbers, and drummers will also occupy roles in another system – the system of social and economic stratification which is indisputably the main regulator of their income, life-style and rank.

Social relationships among
Sikhs are not defined by caste,
but by a stratification of
families, their honor and
their coalitions.

Peoples of the Indian subcontine

SCALE 0 0

Within the Indian subcontinent are an unparalleled variety of ethnic groups, culture patterns and styles of living. While in most other parts of the world rising civilizations replaced those that had preceded them, and conquering populations either eliminated or absorbed earlier inhabitants, in India the arrival of new immigrants and the spread of their way of life did not necessarily cause the disappearance of earlier and materially less advanced communities. In India the old and the new have persisted side by side.

This exceptional mixing of people and cultures has been only partly due to the great size of the subcontinent and the dearth of communications. More important has been an attitude basic to Indian ideology which has accepted variety of cultural forms as natural and immutable, and has not considered assimilation to one cultural pattern in any way desirable. This accounts for the fact that only a few decades ago primitive tribes, subsisting like stone-age man on the wild produce of the forest, could be found within a few hours' journey from historic centers of advanced civilization. Even today there is an unbridged gap between the conservative peasantry of the remoter areas and the partly westernized society of modern industrial towns.

In present-day India cultural contrasts are matched by equally profound differences in the physical make-up of the various ethnic groups. The racial diversities strike even the most casual observer, and reflect the composite nature of a population formed by successive waves of invaders who entered the subcontinent from the north-west as well as the north-east. In India three major racial divisions of mankind overlap and dovetail. The population of the north and of large parts of peninsular India constitutes the easternmost branch of the europoid (or caucasoid) race. In the Himalayan regions and all along India's eastern borders dwell people of the mongoloid race, and among the tribal populations of middle and southern India there is an element which anthropologists describe as veddoid or proto-australoid. The term veddoid is derived from the name of a small and now almost extinct jungle tribe, the Vedda, who live in the interior of Ceylon. Veddoids are dark-skinned and often curly haired; their faces are roundish or heart-shaped with broad, depressed noses and low foreheads. They represent one of the most archaic sections of humanity, extend into some of the accessible regions of South-east Asia and link the oldest surviving racial stratum of India with the Australian aborigines.

As in other parts of the world there are no clear dividing lines between the various racial types. While in certain castes and tribes europoid, mongoloid or veddoid elements predominate, other populations evince a confusing mixture of racial characteristics resulting no doubt from interbreeding. The people of some parts of southern India whose facial features resemble those of Europeans have a skin-color of darkest brown seen elsewhere only in Negroes. The pygmies of the Andaman Islands, which belong politically to India, are of negroid type.

Although there must have been some interbreeding ever since the second millennium BC when the light-skinned Aryans invaded India and encountered there a darker-skinned indigenous population, in many regions of India distinct racial types persist side by side. Their co-existence over centuries, if not millennia, indicates the strong barriers dividing community from community, and standing in the way of intermarriage.

Racial distinctions also affect present-day social relations. Color prejudice is not a monopoly of the 'white' race. In India a light skin is a social asset. The man of europoid type feels superior to the dark-skinned, curly haired, broad-faced aboriginal. Unconsciously he equates these primitive features with cultural backwardness. Yet India is one of the few countries where multi-racial situations have not caused social and political tensions. This is probably due to caste barriers which prevent social contacts irrespective of color and racial type.

The languages, like the racial groups, of the subcontinent belong to several distinct and totally unconnected groups. There are four major language families – Indo-Aryan, Dravidian, Tibeto-Burman and Austro-Asiatic – each of which is divided into numerous mutually unintelligible languages, some of them spoken by only a few hundred people. According to official census reports there are over 15,000 Indian languages. Many of these are tribal dialects, which have never been reduced to writing and are gradually giving way to regionally more important literate languages.

Three hundred and twenty-two million people who live in a compact block in most of northern India and much of middle India speak Indo-Aryan languages, which belong to the same language family as the languages of Europe. Widely used languages in this group include Hindi, Urdu, Punjabi, Marathi, Bengali and Assamese. Hindi, which is spoken by 133 millions, aspires to be a national language, designed ultimately to replace English.

Dravidian, with some one hundred and seven million speakers, is the next largest language family. Unlike the Indo-Aryan languages the Dravidian languages, which are very diversified, are peculiar to India. All attempts to trace historic connections with other languages have failed. Dravidian languages include written languages with a literature reaching back into the first millennium AD, such as Tamil, as well as unwritten tribal languages such as Gondi. The Dravidian languages are concentrated today in the southern part of the peninsula where Tamil, Telugu, Kannada and Malayalam are the dominant regional languages. It is most likely that Dravidian tongues were also once spoken in parts of northern India, but were later displaced by those of the invading Aryans.

Wedged between Aryan and Dravidian languages is another group of tribal languages, the Munda, which

IRAN

A

C von Fürer-Haimendorf

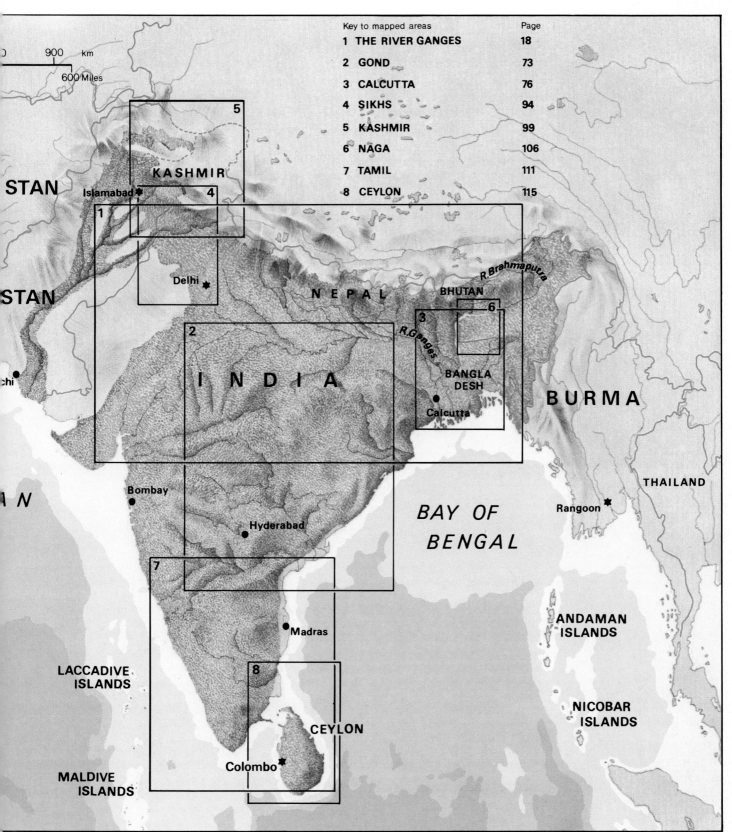

900 km

600 Miles

KASHMIR

Islamabad

STAN

STAN

Delhi

NEPAL

R. Brahmaputra

BHUTAN

6

3

R. Ganges

2

INDIA

BANGLA DESH

Calcutta

BURMA

chi

Bombay

Hyderabad

BAY OF BENGAL

Rangoon

THAILAND

7

Madras

ANDAMAN ISLANDS

LACCADIVE ISLANDS

8

CEYLON

NICOBAR ISLANDS

Colombo

MALDIVE ISLANDS

constitute the western branch of the Austro-Asiatic languages. An eastern branch, the Mon-Khmer language group, are confined to a relatively small area and are spoken in the highlands south of the Brahmaputra valley. The Munda languages, none of which are written, are spoken by some six million people, mainly the tribal people of Bihar and Orissa. Many scholars consider them the most ancient surviving language-group in India. Their principal connections point to countries to the east of India. It is probable that Munda speakers reached India from the north-east long before the Aryans streamed into the country from the north-west.

Tibeto-Burman languages spoken in India and Bangladesh are similarly an extension of a language family centered in Tibet and Burma. They are closely associated with mongoloid people and account for more than half the unwritten tribal languages in India.

There can be no doubt that the peoples who speak these languages of unconnected groups, with connections pointing to diametrically opposed geographical directions, are heirs to different cultural traditions, although by contact and borrowing some of the traditions may have spread across language boundaries throughout the subcontinent. Nevertheless India remains a land of many languages and dialects which are mutually unintelligible. This linguistic diversity is one of the greatest threats to political unity. Language is the main focal point for regional patriotism.

After the end of British rule, which imposed a political unity that had never before existed in India's history, there arose a strong popular demand for the administrative units to be reorganized according to the language spoken by the majority of the population. 'Linguistic states' were created, with the result that the majority of Telugu or Gujarati speakers were included within substantially autonomous states. Language has thus tended to determine political structure. The multi-lingual, multi-cultural and multi-racial Republic of India is divided into sectors which are largely mono-lingual and ideally mono-cultural.

This raises a question of whether linguistic and cultural areas tend to coincide. If India's cultures are classified on a regional basis language is certainly an important means of identifying groups of people. But simply to equate language and culture is in some parts of India an over-simplification. There are regions where uniformity of language does not imply uniformity of culture. The Hindu castes of Bengal or Maharashtra share a number of distinctive customs and practices, styles of dress and dietary habits, as well as a common folklore and literature. But in the Telugu-speaking state of Andhra or in Kerala populations range from city dwellers with a sophisticated brahmanical tradition to semi-nomadic primitive jungle tribes. Although they speak the same language these people have little else in common. Indeed they belong to widely divergent cultural traditions. If

cultural levels differ so fundamentally even within a linguistic area it is well nigh impossible to define a specifically Indian style of living.

The physical environment too is very diverse. It ranges from the humid tropical rain-forests of Kerala and Assam to the desert landscape of Rajasthan. And it has given rise to an equally great variety of settlement patterns. Compact villages, with all the houses standing in streets or in separate clusters, are typical of the Gangetic plains and parts of the Deccan, while dispersed settlements, which can hardly be described as villages, characterize the coastal regions of Kerala. Houses range from the often renewed grass-thatched bamboo huts to solid, tiled buildings of stone which may last for centuries.

Not only does the means of subsistence of semi-nomadic forest tribes contrast with that of settled peasant farmers; there is also the fundamental distinction between dry farming and the cultivation of rice on artificially irrigated fields. Whereas wheat, barley and millet are the staple crops of the dry regions, rice is the indispensable base of the diet of such areas as Bengal and Assam. Differences in the traditional systems of land tenure, which have persisted throughout the period of British rule, are just as important.

There are striking differences too, in the kinship systems of the various regions. The family structure of Aryan speakers in north India is fundamentally different from that of the Dravidian people of the south. Even within these major groups there is no uniformity in marriage patterns. In Kerala, for instance, the patriarchal family system, which traditionally allows a man to marry several wives, co-exists with a system in which property and family name are inherited in the female line, and women could have several husbands without living with any of them. Both types of marriage had the sanction of tradition, although modern trends favor the patriarchal family, and polyandry is waning.

There is overall an underlying unity in the principles determining the structure of society. Wherever Hinduism extends its influence the structure of Indian society is characterized by a large number of permanently unequal, hierarchic groups. These hereditary groups, commonly known as castes, stand to each other in a traditionally fixed position. There is virtually no mobility for individuals from one caste to the other. A man from a village in Kerala, in the extreme south of the peninsula, would have no difficulty understanding the structure of a village community in a Himalayan valley. In both regions the Brahman priestly caste stands at the apex of the social order; untouchable laborers and craftsmen occupy the lowest strata. This system of ranked castes (see pages 44 to 53) invests Indian society with a cohesion and uniformity wherever the philosophy of Hinduism prevails.

For most of its recorded history the Indian subcontinent was dominated by Hindu ideas. Buddhism in its land of origin was no more than an interlude. Even when Muslim invaders established their political rule over much of northern India, the indigenous social system survived. In some respects it even assimilated the newcomers, with the result that there are caste-like groupings also among Muslims although the very idea of the inequality of castes is inconsistent with the traditional ideology of Islam.

Religion, next to language, has been one of the main divisive factors. The partition of the subcontinent into two states of India and Pakistan was the ultimate result of a long-standing antagonism between Hindus and Muslims. A sizeable Muslim minority remains, however, living in close proximity to Hindu communities. The members of the two religious groups usually speak the same language and share many features of the local culture. In areas where Muslim rule continued even during the British period, as in the princely state of Hyderabad where the ruler and politically dominant élite were Muslim, there was a wider gap between Hindu and Muslim traditions and styles of living, extending even to differences of language. While the Hindus spoke Telugu or another regional tongue, the Muslims spoke, as they still do, Urdu, the composite north Indian language which is written in Arabic script and was the main medium of communication in the Mogul empire.

Sikhs, Parsees and Christians are other minority groups who profess distinct religions. Of these only Sikhism, founded in the 15th century as a reaction against the rigidity of the caste system, is an offshoot of Hinduism. It failed in its attempt to unite Hindus and Muslims in an ideology acceptable to both. In time it became an established religion, with its followers organized on the model of Hindu castes. The Parsees, on the other hand, are descendants of .immigrants from Persia who settled in western India. Their religion, Zorastrianism, is one of the few survivals of the ancient pre-Islamic faith of Persia. Parsees are a distinct, closely knit mercantile community confined mainly to Bombay and some towns of Gujarat. Christian communities of varying antiquity are, on the other hand, spread over many parts of India. Apart from their religious practices and convictions Indian Christians follow the social and cultural patterns of where they live.

By maintaining links with their co-religionists in other countries Muslims and Christians contributed significantly to Indian civilization. They brought new ideas and material achievements to the subcontinent. The proudest monuments of the Muslim period are the magnificent Mogul buildings of northern India. The most fruitful contribution of Christianity is an education system largely developed by Christian missionaries.

The island of Ceylon, recently renamed Sri Lanka, is in some respects an extension of the Indian subcontinent without, however, duplicating in detail the social and cultural pattern of India. The main ethnic components of its population and its classical culture stem undoubtedly from India, but its position as an island on the sea routes east and west has exposed it also to other influences.

About 70 per cent of the population speak Sinhalese, an Aryan tongue related to the languages of northern India. Most Sinhalese speakers are Buddhist. Language and religion divide them from the Tamil, an overflow from the Indian mainland who constitute some 22 per cent of the total population. They have lived in the northern part of the island since the second century BC whereas the so-called Indian Tamil in the central highlands are relatively recent 19th century immigrants who came as plantation laborers and remained isolated from the rest of the Ceylonese. The Moor community, who speak a mixture of Tamil and Arabic, are descendants of Islamic settlers. Other minority groups are Eurasians, Burghers (descendants of Dutch settlers) and Malays.

The Buddhist doctrine, in its original form known as Theravada or Hinayana Buddhism, has been the basis of Ceylon's cultural life for more than two millennia. Orders of celibate monks, centered in large well-endowed monasteries, are the traditional intellectual élite. While their influence diminished during British rule it revived in the train of the nationalist upsurge of recent years. Side by side with Buddhism there exists among the Sinhalese a folk religion which is distinct in essence and in external forms from the pure doctrine professed by the monks. It is based on a cult of deities and demons, and shares certain features with Hinduism. Both this folk religion and Theravada Buddhism are of great antiquity, and must have co-existed for at least two thousand years.

Apart from an ancient tribe of jungle dwellers known as Vedda, who are now reduced to a few hundred individuals on the point of merging with the lower strata of the peasantry, there are among the Sinhalese speakers several social groups that resemble Indian castes. Although the idea of permanently unequal sections of society is foreign to Buddhist ideology, these groups are arranged in a hierarchic order, and some have occupational associations. The most prominent of these 'castes' includes a landed gentry which has produced many of the country's leading political figures. Next in rank and power today is a caste originally confined to the fishing villages of the west coast, who catch and sell fish and have attained a powerful position in the economic life of the country.

Caste divisions within the Buddhist, Sinhalese-speaking majority population are relatively insignificant compared to the distinctions which separate them from the Hindu, Tamil and the Muslim, Christian and other minorities whose cultural identities have been shaped by traditions imported from overseas countries.

South Asia has undergone many changes in its 2,500 year old recorded history. But from the common matrix which gave birth to Hinduism and Buddhism there is a distinct cultural atmosphere which sets the subcontinent apart from the rest of the world.

Picture sequence: the Ganges Indian civilization

High in the Himalayas at the first temple on the river a *sadhu*, holy man, raises the waters of the sacred Ganges towards the rising sun.

Hinduism

In almost any bazaar in India you can buy a small oblong paper booklet, rather like a collection of tram tickets. This book lists in Sanskrit all the 1,108 names of the Ganges, printed metrically so that they can be chanted devotionally. For the River Ganges – Ganga Ma or Mother Ganges – is to Hindus the most holy river on earth; and if a Hindu chants 'Ganga, Ganga' even 100 leagues away from the river, he atones for the sins he committed in his three previous existences. The Hindus' many names for the Ganges reflect their faith in the powers of the waters and their dependence on the fertility the waters bring. They call the Ganges The Pure, The Eternal, The Light Amid the Darkness, The Cow Which Gives Much Milk, The Liberator, The Destroyer of Poverty and Sorrow, and The Creator of Happiness.

To bathe in the Ganges, to make a pilgrimage to one of the holy places, perhaps in the icy mountains, and to have one's ashes scattered on its current are the desires of every Hindu. Mysteriously, though the Ganges is polluted by sewage and decomposing corpses, it does not carry cholera, outlasts other water, and has other remarkable properties. But when the early Aryan invaders entered India from the west they came first to the Indus; it was only later that they recognized the Ganges as Sursari – the river of the gods. So the Aryans called the peoples of the River Indus, and the peoples who lived and worshipped like them, the Hindus.

The Hindus are a people first, a religion second, much like Jews in the modern world: the word 'Hindu' is primarily a social term. The Hindu is best defined by a process of elimination: he is an inhabitant of India who does not profess to belong to another religion – Buddhism, Jainism, Christianity, or some tribal religion, for example. Hindus themselves emphasize purity of birth. One must be born a Hindu; one cannot achieve it; nor, indeed, was being a Hindu ever thrust upon anyone, for Hindus have never tried to make converts.

As Hinduism is more a social system than a doctrine, a man is a Hindu because of what he does rather than what he believes. The ancient, classical definition of a Hindu is one who adheres to the four classes and four stages, and who believes in the Vedas. The allusion to the four classes refers to the hierarchical structure of the four classes (Brahman, noble, bourgeois and servant) around which the more specific, practical and intricate workings of the caste system are set, and to the four progressive stages of life: student, householder, forest-dweller and ascetic. The Hindu system clearly aims above all for a social world in which, although all varieties of human experience may be realized, they may not all be realized at once, nor indeed all by one person. The caste system recognizes the equal value – though not of course the equal prestige – to society as a whole of all tasks from the highest (the religious functions of the Brahman) to the lowest (the impure and abhorred tasks of the butcher and sewage worker). Each person has his own particular duty, his own *dharma*, a thread which contributes to the 17

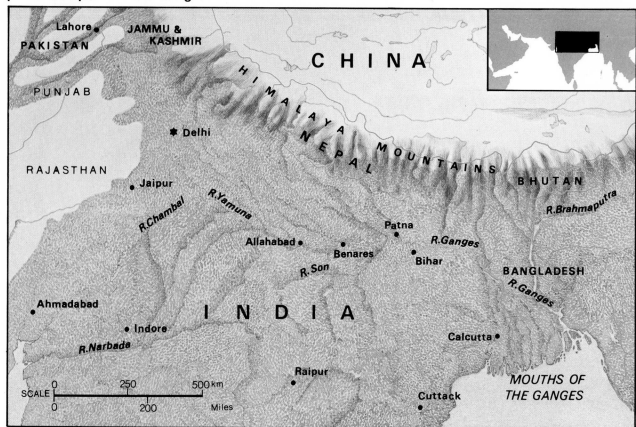

larger fabric of the social order or *dharma*. Among the four stages of life the second stage, of the householder, allows a man to indulge fully in the sensual, materialistic existence which has made the *Kamasutra*, the splendor of the Maharajas, and the erotic temples of the Khajuraho so notorious, but the fourth stage, of the ascetic, also allows the ascetic yogi to develop the complete indifference to physical phenomena which has made the fire-walkers, self-mutilators, and Maharshis equally renowned.

The second part of the Hindu definition of a Hindu – that he should believe in the Vedas – has, contrary to appearances, no doctrinal implications. For the Vedas were composed in an archaic form of Sanskrit more than 3,000 years ago, and today only a scattering of learned priests and erudite European scholars can actually read them. The Hindu, therefore, does not believe the Vedas, he merely believes *in* the Vedas. Indeed Hinduism is often taken in a more specific sense to mean the sectarian religion which developed in India at the beginning of the Christian era, in direct contrast with Brahmanism, the Vedic religion from which Hinduism developed. The actual text which contains the doctrine which most orthodox Hindus believe is the *Bhagavad Gita*, the Song of God, written more than 1,000 years after the Vedas. The *Gita* is a remarkable work of synthesis and resolves many apparent contradictions of the religion, a tradition on the one hand, of sacrificial ritual and, on the other

18

A personification of the river, the goddess Ganga is depicted riding a crocodile, holding an urn of water and a lotus flower.

(Right) As he has done daily for 14 years the *sadhu* bathes at the source of the Ganges, the Gangotri glacier, 13,000 feet up in the Himalayas.

picture sequence: the Ganges

Pilgrims struggle up mountain paths to bathe at the Ganges' source. Hindus regard many rivers as holy, but the Ganges is most sacred of all.

(Bottom) The upper reaches are too turbulent for rigid craft. A lumberman propels himself towards jammed logs on an inflated buffalo hide.

(Right) A *sadhu* meditates on rocks known in legend as the hair of the god Shiva, in whose locks the Ganges was caught in its descent to earth.

phallic emblem of the God Shiva. In an earlier period the Hindus regarded the historical Buddha as an incarnation of their god Vishnu – a form which, they quickly added, Vishnu assumed in order to teach a false doctrine, to thin out the uncouth crowds of heaven and to make heaven exclusive to and therefore more pleasant for true believers.

Such a variety of beliefs is due partly to the intentions of those who formulated classical Hindu doctrine, but also to the assimilation of more than 232 million people of many origins – Aryan, Dravidian, tribal, and foreign (Greeks, central Asians, Arabs, Europeans, and many others). This racial mixture has also added fuel to the fire of Hindu belief in the importance of purity. For Hindus recognize not only the temporary impurities which in most societies characterize the great life transitions (birth, menstruation, marriage, death), but also the permanent impurities which result from one's birth and occupation – the impurities of caste. The extremes of purity and impurity impose peculiar restrictions on Indian society. Brahmans of certain castes – primarily the Kulins – were considered so pure that their women could marry only men of a class much smaller than their own. Since it is essential for a Hindu to find husbands for all his daughters many infant Kulin girls were killed rather than left to face a fate of barrenness or defilement, worse than death. Untouchables (Harijan), on the other hand, were considered so impure that the mere sight of them, or even contact with their shadows, would pollute anyone of higher status. Yet only untouchables could be employed for the most defiling, and therefore often the most intimate, tasks of daily life, such as washing menstrual cloths or cleaning out lavatories. Extremes of this sort have been largely eliminated by British and modern Indian legal reforms, but the mental attitudes persist. 'Kulinism' is gone, but marriages are still arranged along strict caste lines. Untouchables are better treated, but deeply ingrained concepts of impurity and defilement may be seen in such idiosyncracies as the employment of high-caste Brahmans as cooks and water-bearers for all lower castes, since the Brahmans are the only ones from whom all castes can accept food.

Fire and water, the elemental purifiers, play a central role in all Hindu rituals. Fire is worshipped in its celestial form (the sun) by every Hindu every day at dawn and sunset, as he recites the ancient Vedic Gayatri hymn to the sun, the only Vedic verse known by most Hindus. Fire is circumambulated seven times by the Hindu marriage couple, and into the cremation fire the Hindu consigns all corpses. Water is used for daily, temporary pollutions. A Hindu bathes many times each day, especially after eating, defecating, seeing an impure sight, or cursing. And water, together with fire, is used at the great rites of passage. If possible, the Hindu recites his Gayatri hymn while immersed in a river, and ashes of the corpse cremated on a burning *ghat* on the river

hand, a philosophy which preaches non-injury to all living creatures. The *Gita* uses the many new concepts not in place of, but in addition to, the old, creating a crazy-quilt of metaphysical patches salvaged from many different historical eras.

Given this elasticity of doctrine, it is not surprising that the legal definition of a Hindu is carefully vague: 'Acceptance of the Vedas with reverence; recognition of the fact that the means or ways to salvation are diverse; and realization of the truth that the number of gods to be worshipped is large, that indeed is the distinguishing feature of Hindu religion.' Salvation in the Hindu context implies above all belief in transmigration of souls and in the possibility of release from the circle of rebirths, each rebirth determined by the individual's *karma* – the fruit of his good or bad actions in previous births. As for the 'number of gods', the Hindus have always worshipped very many different gods, identifying their own gods with Christ (which early Christian missionaries in India found very frustrating) and Queen Victoria of England – who would surely not have been amused to have discovered statues of herself bowing in silent reverence before the

A score of rivers are longer
or mightier than the Ganges,
but none is as holy; it was
the sacred heart of India
long before Christ's birth.

banks are placed in its waters. Rivers have always been holy for Hindus, a people whose name originates in a Persian term, calling them 'the people of the river'. The waters of the Ganges, Jamuna, Narbada, Kistna and Sarasvati are particularly holy. Places where rivers flow together are more sacred yet, and Allahabad (Prayaga), where three sacred rivers meet, is the most auspicious of all. Water from sacred rivers, especially the Ganges, is bottled and used for sacred and medicinal purposes throughout India, and pilgrimages to and along sacred rivers bring great merit to the worshipper.

The Hindu universe is characterized by fire and water. The universe is said to have developed out of the cosmic waters when the germ of fire was sown in them. Then came the first of the four Hindu ages, which have been given names derived from throws of a dice, in keeping with the Hindu view of life as a sport played by the gods. The first age, the Krita Yuga, was the best. Then men fell prey to lust and greed, and the world degenerated. The present age, the Kali Yuga, is the lowest. When it ends the universe will be destroyed by fire and flood – and out of the waters Krita Yuga will begin again.

Hindu ritual takes place on two levels: in the home and in the temple. By far the most important of the domestic rituals is the sacrifice to the deceased ancestors of an offering of balls of cooked rice and libations of water. This ritual, called *Sraddha*, takes place for the first time soon after death, and is often an expensive and elaborate ceremony. After that more simple, daily ceremonies suffice, but these must be performed by the eldest son of the dead man or the dead man will find no rest. This means that Hindus place great emphasis on male heirs. In most homes, daily offerings of flowers, incense, or food are also made at small shrines dedicated to one of the great Hindu gods. This simple ritual, known as *puja*, has largely replaced the more elaborate sacrifices which characterized Vedic worship in the ancient Brahmanic period. Small local shrines dedicated to serpents, trees, fertility gods or village deities are also given *puja* of this sort.

At the temple, the center of communal religion, groups of priests make daily offerings to the great Hindu gods. There are also recitations of sacred texts, readings from the Vedas and the *Bhagavad Gita* as well as from later, more popular, collections of myths, legends and local stories magnifying the sanctity of the temple and its shrine. Priests from the great local temple are also called upon to provide the religious education of young men of the upper castes and to perform the special rites of passage for the more influential families of the area, while more humble local shrines will supply less prestigious priests for members of the lower castes. Great temples at particularly holy places are objects of pilgrimage and sites of annual festivals which attract many thousands of worshippers. Of these, the temple of Vishnu at Vrindaban, the Jagannatha ('Juggernaut') temple of Vishnu at Puri, the temple of the goddess Minakshi at Madurai, and the

shrines of Shiva at Benares are most famous.

Most temples are dedicated to one of the two great gods, Vishnu and Shiva, each of whom is regarded by his worshippers as the supreme god who controls and indeed embodies all other gods. Worship is performed in the spirit of *bhakti*, or devotion, the love of the worshipper for his god and of the god for the worshipper, an irrational, often unconventional emotion which may rise above and replace the traditional forces of *dharma* and *karma*, even the flow of time and fate. Vishnu is worshipped in a number of different incarnations, or avatars, of which the two most popular are the prince Rama and the cow-herd Krishna. Rama – the hero of the great Sanskrit epic, the *Ramayana* – is the epitome of the good king, the good son, the good brother, the good husband, and Hindus never tire of praising Rama's virtues and recounting his deeds of valor: how he and his ally Hanuman, the monkey king, built a bridge to the island of Sri Lanka (Ceylon) to rescue Rama's wife, Sita, when she had been stolen away by the demon Ravana. Krishna, on the other hand, charms by his mischief rather than by his virtue. As a baby, Krishna steals butter and feeds it to the monkeys, and as a hand-

22

A third of India's nearly 600m people live in the fertile river plain, their crops watered and their souls refreshed by *Ganga Ma*.

(Over page) Millions of pilgrims visit Allahabad at the confluence of the Ganges and Yamuna every 12th year for the Kumbh Mela festival.

Newly married couples like this veiled bride and her husband, symbolically tied together, make the customary wedding visit to the river.

some young man he dances in the moonlight with the wives of the cow-herds. His erotic appeal has inspired many beautiful poems in which the worshipper assumes the emotional attitude of a woman longing for her lover, Krishna. Shiva is a more mysterious god, incorporating in his many diverse cults both the most arcane refinements of Indian philosophical speculation and the orgiastic rituals of the tribal people of pre-Vedic India. He is the god of ascetics, whose holy city is Benares, but also the god whose *linga*, or phallus is worshipped. He is the god of Brahmans, but also the god of the Kapalikas or Skull-bearers, a cult of wandering naked beggars who are despised by most orthodox Hindus. Two of Shiva's sons are objects of worship in their own right: Skanda, the six-headed god of war, whose cult is particularly prominent in south India, and Ganesha, the elephant-headed god of scribes and remover of obstacles, who is worshipped by everyone in need of crafty assistance, but particularly by merchants and intellectuals throughout the country.

Although the Vedic pantheon of gods, to which both Vishnu and Shiva trace minor elements of their cults, was, like all Indo-European religions, patrilineal (based on descent through the male line) and male-orientated, there was in the land invaded by the Indo-Aryans a thriving cult of the great Goddess, as well as numerous 23

shrines to minor goddesses. Classical Hinduism, with its emphasis upon ritual chastity and its consequent misogyny, with its ingrained belief that lust and women are the source of all evil, regarded these goddesses with a jaundiced eye. But to accommodate the demands of popular Hinduism, with its emphasis on fertility and the need for sons, with its unquenchable celebration of the pleasures of the flesh, a characteristic synthesis was fashioned. The great Aryan gods were given Dravidian goddesses for their wives, the goddesses' power was recognized but, to satisfy the misgivings of classical misogynism, the emphasis was placed on the destructive aspect of this power. Thus the Goddess Devi was said to appear as Lakshmi, the wife of Vishnu and goddess of prosperity, or as Parvati, the wife of Shiva and daughter of the mountain Himalaya. Although in both these roles she was a beautiful, modest wife, far more stress was laid upon her aspect as Kali, the great black goddess of death, the drinker of blood, garlanded with human skulls, who danced wildly on the corpse of her husband Shiva. The cult of Devi, even more than that of Vishnu or Shiva, has been subject to local variations. Sometimes she is the bringer of smallpox, sometimes a young human girl, and sometimes a benevolent tree-spirit. In Bengal, where she is known as Durga, the ceremony of Durga Puja takes place for ten days in the fall. On the last night the images of Durga are taken from their shrines and set afloat on the river, majestically and silently lit by candles. The darker side of the Goddess is also catered for in Calcutta, a city which derives its very name from Kalighat, the shrine of Kali, where goats are beheaded and offered up at the altar. This ceremony is, ironically, strongly reminiscent of the ancient, pre-Hindu Vedic ritual of animal beheading which, theoretically and historically, underlies Hindu worship, although in fact the slaughters at Kalighat horrify most orthodox, high-caste Hindus. Another power of the Goddess is celebrated in Tantric Hinduism which, like a black mass, utilizes for its worship those very elements which are anathema to a Hindu.

The untamed side of Hinduism expressed in this worship of the Goddess also asserts itself in the safety-valve offered by the festival of Holi celebrated throughout India every spring. At this time all the normal, restrictive social barriers are broken, and members of all castes douse one another with red water which may be a ritual euphemism for the blood saturnalia of an earlier era. At the other extreme, modern sects such as the Arya Samaj and Brahma Samaj have attempted to purge Hinduism of its more barbaric elements in order to make it palatable to more western-oriented Indians. These ancient and modern tendencies which might threaten to tear apart the very underpinnings of any other major religion are easily accommodated side by side in Hinduism, which strives, above all, to provide a god for every need, good or evil, a divine sanction for every human possibility, worldly or spiritual.

History

arrying the hem of his lungi to keep it from the dirt, and accompanied by two western visitors, a Brahman farmer follows a path along the top of an embankment between two bright green paddy fields. Some way ahead a group of people approaching from the other direction stop and clamber laboriously down the side of the embankment; they wait below until the farmer and his friends have passed. The farmer explains that these people are untouchables; technically, they are supposed to keep 20 feet away from a passing high-caste person. But, he adds wistfully, the old rules are weakening and the 20 feet are often not strictly observed. This is a tiny episode of a type that occurs thousands of times daily in the villages of south India.

This scene, which seems more fundamental the more one reflects upon Indian history, shows the continuing contrast between two worlds – the official world of the educated élite and its culture, often called the great tradition, and the village world, with its folk culture and limited horizons, often called the little tradition.

In the great tradition – among many educated people, and according to Indian law – untouchability is something to be finally done away with, something now legally abolished. In the little tradition, at least in the south where such observances are stricter, untouchability is often a matter of unquestioned everyday practice.

This sort of contrast, between the world of metropolitan man and the village peasant, has been repeated many times over at the various stages of Indian history. It is not a contrast between two unrelated traditions. On the contrary, throughout history, village affairs have influenced the culture and politics of empires, and the trend of events at royal courts has had a far-reaching effect, even if indirect and unintended, on village life. The point is that the relationship between these traditions is necessarily subtle, mutable and insidious.

This interaction may be seen at the very beginning of Indian history (see pages 130–133). Conventionally, the record begins about midway through the second millennium BC with the immigration of the Aryan tribes who came through the north-west passes of modern Pakistan. There were, indeed, already highly developed urban cultures in north-western India known through fascinating archaeological finds at many sites, notably Mohenjo Daro and Harappa. But this civilization collapsed in mysterious circumstances. Very possibly the nomadic Aryans rode through the cities as conquerors, their battle-cries ringing among the proud buildings where now there is an empty waste. We can only guess.

Yet the Aryans, the new conquering race – *Arya* is Sanskrit for 'noble' – could not maintain their culture unchanged in its new environment, nor could their subjects resist the influence of Aryan traditions. Many pre-Aryan communities were brought into the fold and adopted Aryan ways, and a new composite culture began to emerge. By 500 BC the immigrants had spread across

26

Ash-covered *sadhus* walk through the crowds to bathe. Sacred threads over their shoulders mark them as members of twice-born castes.

The sign on his forehead shows he is a worshipper of the mysterious god Shiva whose cults range from the orgiastic to the mystical.

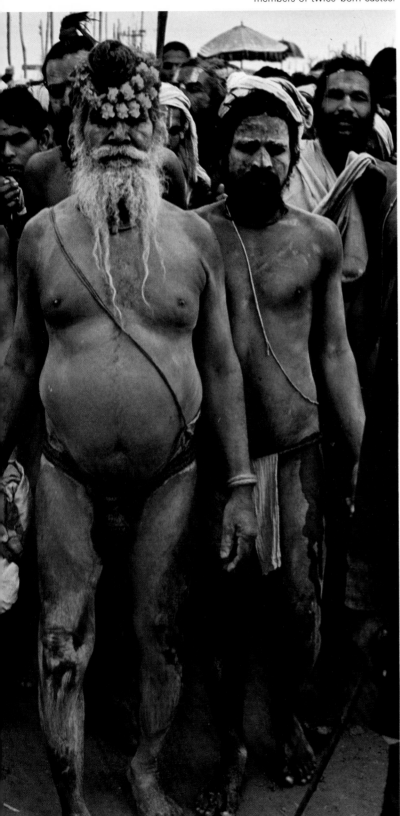

the north of India from the Punjab to the Ganges valley, forsaking their pastoral, nomadic way of life for settled agriculture. We know of them from their religious hymns and sacred formulae, the Vedas, originally passed on by word of mouth and later congealing into the corpus of Vedic literature.

The subsequent evolution of Hinduism shows signs of the compromise of Aryan religion with the local traditions of the pre-Aryan tribes – Dravidian-speaking, Australoid, Negrito – an ethnic mosaic linked with other parts of Asia – with their local cults of earth gods or goddesses bearing associations of darkness, snakes, mystery and sacrifice. This inference is partly speculative, but such features can be seen in the local cults of modern Indian practice, most strongly where the impact of the 'great tradition' originating with the Aryans has been lightest, and also in the primitive regions of adjoining areas of Asia and the islands. Thus we can see that the official culture of the conquerors was arbitrarily superimposed on a medley of linked cultures which extended over a much larger area (including South-east Asia and southern China) than that brought under direct Aryan 27

picture sequence: the Ganges

Four peasant women in Bihar huddle together against the monsoon; they rejoice in the storm for it means a good crop for the coming year.

His boat hastily pulled onto the river bank, a man runs from the dust storm which heralds the monsoon rains.

political influence. With the gradual movement of Aryan peoples by land their influence spread, century by century, across the whole subcontinent, but their traditions were increasingly diluted by contact with those of pre-Aryan peoples. And in the latter part of the first millennium BC many of the features of Indian life that have been familiar ever since began to take shape. Settled kingdoms appeared. New leisured classes grew. And the Brahman, custodians of religious tradition and performers of sacrifices, were supported by the pious offerings of others. Non-orthodox sects appeared, partly as a reaction against routine religious practices and offerings without deep religious feeling. The greatest of these sects was that founded in the 6th century BC by the Buddha, a member of a princely family who lived in the Himalayan foothills of present-day Nepal.

The Buddha's teachings stressed simplicity and the right approach to the task of seeking enlightenment rather than correctly performed rituals. This went counter to the hierarchical spirit embodied in Hindu custom and caste. His teachings had a deep influence on much of northern India for centuries.

28

The second Mauryan emperor, Ashoka (269-232 BC), was converted to Buddhism and had a pillar inscribed with his repentance of his former violence. In his time inscribed rocks and pillars were finished with a remarkable polish unknown to stoneworkers before or since. There has been much discussion by historians about the nature of his empire. Although it was probably not the highly organized totalitarian state that it has been thought, the direct influence of Ashoka and his Buddhist message spread far and wide.

In the following centuries the empire of the Mauryas gradually dwindled like dying embers. Other kingdoms and little empires rose and fell. Many new kingdoms were carved out in the north-west during the last few centuries BC and the early centuries AD by waves of invaders – Greeks, Scythians and others. In the first millennium AD, the classical period when Sanskrit literature, stone temple building, and the dominant Hindu cults of Shiva and Vishnu rose and flourished, more empires were founded. Chief among them was the 4th and 5th century north Indian empire of the Guptas, who were conquerors and patrons of the arts.

Muslim rulers were originally invaders, often of largely Turkish descent, and professing Persian culture – the literature and especially the architecture of the Moguls show strong Persian influence – who came by the north-western passes from Afghanistan. The early invaders, from the 10th to 12th centuries, were raiders drawn by the hope of plundering the rich treasures of Indian temples and courts. The so-called slave dynasty (1206-1290) represented the beginning of Muslim empire based in India, although the rulers were foreigners living in military fortresses rather than native emperors. From the 16th century to the 18th the Moguls presided over an empire which, at its height under Akbar included most of India, leaving only some independent kingdoms in the south. Then came the British.

It would be wrong to foster the supposition that the Muslim period of Indian history was in some sense wholly Muslim, or that Muslim kingdoms in India were totally different from Hindu ones. Nor were they entirely alien and ephemeral and therefore without effect. Indeed Muslim culture had a big impact on the arts and sciences, and much of it was absorbed by the Hindu élite, but it would be wrong to regard the India encountered by the Europeans as a homogeneous Muslim empire wholly regulated from the top. When the Mogul power at the top crumbled away, as it did in the 18th century – although nominal Mogul rulers continued as pensioners of the British until 1858 – there was not complete anarchy. Local powers continued, imbued to a greater or lesser extent with Mogul traditions and legitimacy.

But it is important to realize that the grid of political geography lay lightly on the rich mosaic of Indian life. Armies came and went; grand capitals were built at prodigious expense, and were abandoned – like Akbar's 29

picture sequence: the Ganges

The demon Rahu causes an eclipse of the sun and all is defiled. When the sun returns Benares pilgrims will again bathe in the sacred river.

(Bottom) His eyes fixed on heaven, a bather prays. Every Hindu wishes to visit Benares; those who die there are taken instantly to Shiva in paradise.

A father teaches his son to pray in the river at Benares, for centuries sanctified by its position on a bend in the river facing the rising sun.

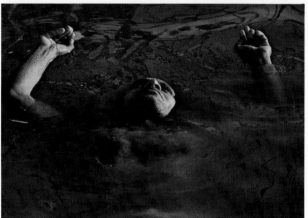

Seated under a straw umbrella
a priest prays. Beside him is
a silver urn for holy river
water, its spout shaped like
the head of a cow.

Fatehpur Sikri which was deserted soon after it was built – for want of a water supply. But in the villages life went its own way, not always the same, and not unresponsive to the ideologies and decrees of rulers, but not swept away by them either. For the villager government was something respected in the abstract for the protection it was supposed to give when required, but resented in the concrete, when it most commonly took the form of the tax collector. An old saying held that the two most dangerous positions to occupy were behind a horse and in front of a government official.

Indian village society has often been described as self-contained and autonomous. In some respects this is true, for the population was scattered, the jungle was thicker and the roads few. However this does not mean that village life was an arcadian idyll of the sort that Gandhi seemed to have had in mind as an ideal. True, land was not scarce, and this meant that rulers and landlords had to take care lest they provoked their dependents too far so that they moved away and cleared land elsewhere, but generally life, with its poor hygiene and lack of security, was nasty, brutish and short. The popular archetype of

the cruel tyrannical ruler or the grasping absentee landlord may not have been always the bogey that first thoughts suggest. But certainly the bribery, corruption and intrigue among members of dominant castes in villages and among lesser officials are likely to have been as great a cause of injustice to the peasants in earlier times as they are known to have been in the 19th century.

We know that in this way the British colonial administration was deprived of much of its legally due revenue and we may guess that the apparent harshness of Muslim demands in earlier centuries was at times similarly tempered in practice. But there is plenty of evidence of real extortion under the Mogul rulers whose administrative system itself encouraged it. Many officials who held rank under the empire, *jagirdar*, were made responsible for the collection of revenue from particular revocable grants of territory, *jagir*, from which they made their living. Since *jagir* were frequently withdrawn and reallocated it was in the interest of each *jagirdar* to bleed as much revenue as possible from his territory while it was his.

So the two related patterns of Indian history continued: one of hard facts like battles and empires, belonging to the official history that is easy to chart with dates and maps; and one of complex, subtle and continuous processes among the mass of the population. The same is true of the period of European dominance.

In 1498 three Portuguese ships reached the south-west coast, seeking Christian converts and spices. This was a turning-point, in a sense. Certainly it had no immediate effect on Indian society as a whole. And for centuries the European trading powers were, in Indian eyes, merely additions to the list of peoples thronging the thoroughfares of the port cities. Portuguese, Dutch, French, British and others too, established trading settlements around the coasts.

Little by little the rivalry between the European traders spilled increasingly into the politics of the surrounding principalities, until in the 18th century the British and French were deeply involved in the affairs of the subcontinent. They trained armies, made treaties and chose their own candidates for Indian thrones. The French, handicapped by a shortage of resources and lack of commitment at home, yielded. In 1757, at Plassey, the forces of the British East India Company under Clive won a victory that brought them direct responsibility for the government of large areas in the north-east.

After this victory, the British East India Company gradually developed from a trading association into an Indian government as well. The company acquired its possessions piecemeal, growing out from the three presidencies of Bengal (where the central government was situated), Madras and Bombay.

Whatever colors the parts of India might have been on the map, British rule was for long superficial. It had to be. There were few roads, communications were 31

Modern India has taken much
power from her princes but the
Maharaja of Benares is a
spiritual leader regarded by
many of his people as a god.

Buried up to his neck in sand
a *sadhu* meditates. Pilgrims
gain spiritual merit by
tossing coins onto the
cloth in front of him.

picture sequence: the Ganges

Smoke from funeral pyres hangs
continually over Benares where
30,000 corpses are cremated
annually, their ashes cast on
the breast of Mother Ganges.

34

To bathe in the Ganges washes
away all guilt. To carry the
waters away brings merit. To
call its name atones for sins
committed in previous lives.

generally poor, and a few thousand European officials were thrown here and there on their own resources to govern many millions. Furthermore in the early 19th century, it took up to two and a half years to get an instruction from London on any matter. Naturally enough the governor-generals at Calcutta took most important decisions themselves, and many more were taken in the other presidencies and acquired territories independently of Calcutta. The Indian empire of the first half of the 19th century looks solid to us in retrospect, but it did not seem so to its servants, who felt they had to proceed cautiously in achieving reforms or making the British presence felt in any way at village level.

So, although the empire did not develop exactly as a result of absent-mindedness, it developed haphazardly from the interaction of various interests. There was the British government which supervised, but did not run, the British East India Company until after the traumatic mutiny of revolt of 1857 when the Company was wound up and the government took direct control. There were also the Court of Directors of the Company, the Governor-General – whose loyalties were divided between government, Company and the people around him in Bengal – Company employees who used their position to make private fortunes, and the local Indian rulers.

Even at the time of independence in 1947 there were still 562 princes who ruled a quarter of the Indian population. They were nominally sovereign but influenced in varying degrees by British representatives.

When we consider how totalitarian the British empire in India really was, it is not surprising that many of the results of British rule were unintentional. Revenue administration systems designed by men with social improvement in mind had the effect of reinforcing Indian élites, whether by establishing a class of big landlords (as by the permanent settlement of Bengal in 1793) or by making new land assessments capable of being manipulated in their own favor by dominant groups in the villages. Developments in the economy and communications had the effect of weakening village autonomy and strengthening local aristocracies. Debt courts favored money lenders and harmed peasants. Flood control works even had the effect of creating malarial swamps.

Western education, above all, had the effect of bringing forth new élite groups in the various provinces, which competed with each other and eventually with the British. The first generation of professional men to constitute a new class was the 19th century *bhadralok* of Bengal. These people began to interest themselves in politics, although not, until the end of the century, with any idea

Divali, the Festival of Lights, greets the new moon in the holy month Kartik (in late October) and pilgrims chant hymns to Krishna.

Two devotees are pulled in a rickshaw through Benares streets, unconcerned by the river surging through the city after heavy monsoon rains.

35

In a sacred book are written the 108 names of the Ganges. Now shrunken before the rains, to her people she is still 'Mother of all that lives'.

(Bottom) A paddle steamer ferrying passengers from Patna to Sonepur in Bihar has an air of British imperial pomp.

What it is to be an Indian

India's 541 million people today are descended from a variety of races. The oldest are negroid aboriginals known as adivasis (first settlers). Then there are the Dravidians, the Aryans, the Mongols, the Semites – and innumerable inter-mixtures of one with the other. Nobody quite knows how many languages and dialects are spoken in India. Fifteen are recognized by the Constitution, but English, which is spoken by less than two per cent of the population, continues to be the chief language of communication between the different States of the Union, in the higher échelons of administration and the Courts of Appeal.

Although the vast majority, 80 per cent, of Indians are Hindus, almost every religion known in the world is practised in India. Next to Indonesia and Bangladesh, India has the third largest population of Muslims (70 million). There are also 13 million Christians, 10 million Sikhs, 4 million Buddhists, 2·5 million Jains, and smaller numbers of Zoroastrians and Jews.

Racial, linguistic and religious divisions are older and more deeply embedded in the Indian mind than the sense of Indian-ness which is less than 150 years old. Let me illustrate this from my own life story.

I was born in a small village now in Pakistan. It was largely inhabited by Muslims. There were a few families of Hindus and Sikhs and some untouchables who lived in a cluster of mud huts, a little removed from our home. An outsider coming to our village would never ask 'Who are you?' but 'What are you?'

The answer would invariably indicate the sub caste and the family to which you belonged; never your name. If the person questioned was a Muslim, he would reply 'We are Waddals or Mastials' (tribes of Muslims of Baluchi extraction who between them owned most of the village land). If the person was Hindu he would reply 'We are Brahman or Khatri or Arora' (a Hindu trading caste). Even Sikhs who claimed that Sikhism did not subscribe to the caste system always replied by naming their subcaste. Thus questioned I would answer 'We are Khuranas (a subsect of Aroras); we live opposite the Gurdwara (Sikh temple).' The untouchables, Hindu and Muslim, would simply admit they were untouchables.

When my parents moved to a neighboring town there was a slight variation in the pattern of enquiry and response. The caste or subcaste was only mentioned if the questioner happened to be of your own religious persuasion. To all others you only stated where you had come from and whether you were Muslim, Hindu or Sikh. And although this town was only 40 miles away from our village, we described ourselves as *pardesis* (foreigners) and talked of our ancestral village with nostalgia as our *vatan* (homeland). Even in town the individual was of little importance; what mattered was religion and, for further identification, village of birth.

When I was twelve my parents moved to Delhi, the

of displacing the British. But then new élites began to appear elsewhere, notably in the center and west of northern India (the homelands of Nehru and Gandhi respectively), reacting against what they saw as the parochialism and complacency of the older generation of mild nationalists. They developed a new, strident and universal nationalism which led, step by step, to an ever-intensifying confrontation with British power.

To leave the story there is to say nothing of the importance on the nationalist scene of Hindu revival, of the emergence of Hindu-Muslim conflict in the 19th century, of the British reaction to nationalism, or indeed of many of the factors directly responsible for the India we know today. But it is enough to show how modern historical writing is turning to the study of the infrastructure of politics, the local social changes – the little tradition in a sense. They are analysing Indian social groups at the level of the province and the district. It is this sort of approach which is most likely to make the India of today and tomorrow comprehensible and help us to guess what sort of loyalties or aspirations might, in the near or remote future, persuade the untouchables on the footpath to stay there, and brush the shoulders of the passing Brahman.

Men haul a boat upstream, hard work when the river is high for, in full flood, the Ganges discharges more water than the Mississippi.

seat of government. For the first time I met people from other parts of India including some who professed religions like Christianity or Zoroastrianism with which I had no prior contact, and who spoke languages I could not understand. I became more conscious of my religious identity but less of my caste and subcaste. At the same time I became aware of the province I came from and the language I spoke. When asked who I was I would reply 'I am a Sikh from the Punjab.' Other boys at school would likewise reply 'I am a Muslim from Bengal' or 'I am a Christian from Kerala.' Even in Delhi I never heard anyone describe himself as an Indian.

The first time I became conscious of being Indian was when I went to university in England. This was not surprising since only Englishmen who had been to India could recognize me as a Sikh or a Punjabi. For the others I was lumped together with the Bengali, Maharashtri and Tamil as an Indian. Like other foreigners living in England we Indians tended to herd together. By then we had also started taking interest in our freedom movement. To present a united front against the English we suppressed our religious and linguistic separateness and insisted that we were Indians. The only group in our midst who had some reservations about being Indian were the Muslims. They had already started thinking in terms of a state of their own. In turn we had our reservations about them.

When I returned home to India the Second World War had begun. There were many pulls on our loyalties. A large majority of Indians, though they sympathized with England and her allies, thought that Indian freedom came first, concern for what happened to the rest of the world later. Most young men with leftist leanings, including myself, were of the view that it was more important to make the world safe for democracy by defeating the fascist power than to have a free India which might soon lose its freedom to Japan or Nazi Germany. By then we also sensed that as soon as the war was over we would get our freedom. The concept of Indianness was again in the crucible. Most of us felt that India should remain one country with its frontiers defined by the extent of British possession and it should contain all our population of 350 million people irrespective of religious, racial or linguistic differences. The only Indians who did not share this view of the future of India were the Muslims. Most of them maintained that Indians were not and never had been one nation and that Muslim majority areas should be separated to form a new Muslim state, Pakistan.

This conflict of views led to extensive rioting which in 1946-47 assumed the proportions of a civil war between the Muslims on the one side and Hindus and Sikhs on the other. The country had to be divided. When the division came I was teaching and practising law in Lahore which fell on the Pakistan side of the dividing line. Practically all the five million or so Hindus and Sikhs

37

(Over page) Built in 1786 as a grain store against famine, the 96-foot high Golghar today attracts streams of visitors to view Patna and the Ganges.

Holy men camp at Sagar Island where the Ganges meets the sea and where, 150 years ago, pilgrims cast their children into the water as sacrifices.

who found themselves in West Pakistan were compelled to leave. So were the Muslims living in India's near north-western states. A total of ten million people crossed frontiers, exchanged homes and properties. Nearly half a million were killed in the riots.

On 15 August 1947, India and Pakistan became independent members of the British Commonwealth of Nations. But for both the question of what precisely being Indian or Pakistani meant remained to be defined. West Pakistan was rid of its non-Muslim population, but East Pakistan (now Bangladesh) a thousand miles away still had 10 million Hindus, Buddhists and Christians. And although 5 million Muslims had migrated from India to Pakistan, more than 60 million still remained in India. India had also to contend with divisive forces generated by differences of language and race.

When considering the Indianness of Indians it is necessary to look back and examine what divided Indians into Muslims and non-Muslims so sharply that it dissected India. History casts a long, dividing shadow between Hinduism and Islam. The shadow is of religion, not of race or language, because Hindus and Muslims are of the same race and speak the same languages.

Arab traders are known to have come to India from time immemorial. Dhows laden with products of the desert – dates and aromatic spices – took advantage of the easterly winds and sailed across the Indian Ocean. These Arabs spent the rainy season in India exchanging their wares for Indian textiles and spices and sailed back to their homes before the winter set in. Some, however, stayed and settled in India.

After the prophet Mohammed (AD 570–632) converted the Arabs to Islam, these traders introduced their new faith into India. Mosques sprang up along the western coast. There is evidence to prove that these early Arab Muslims were made more than welcome by the local Hindus, who gave them daughters in marriage. Descendants of these ancient traders are still found in large communities in Malabar, the present-day state of Kerala. They are known as *moplahs* from the Malayalam word *mapilla* meaning son-in-law.

The amicable relationship between Hindus and Muslims changed abruptly when India began to be invaded from the north-west by Muslim armies. Early in the 8th century the 17 year-old Mohammed Bin Qasim overran Sind. From 1000 AD Mahmud of Ghazna began his invasions of India. He destroyed Hindu temples. He put thousands of Hindus to the sword and made a pastime of raising pyramids of the skulls of infidels. He was only the first of a long line of Muslim idol-breakers.

There were peaceful interludes in these centuries of persecution, the most notable being the reign of Akbar, who ruled India from 1556 to 1605. Akbar abolished discrimination against subjects of different faiths, elevated Hindus to high positions and entered into matrimonial alliances with Hindu princes. Akbar's name is honored with the title Akbar the Great. Aurangzeb, who is praised by Muslim historians for his piety and the firmness with which he dealt with his non-Muslim subjects, is abominated by the Hindus.

It is little wonder that the Hindus began to look upon Muslims as tyrants and shunned those Indians who accepted Islam. It took many long years of suffering and humiliation before the Hindus were able to hit back. The Mahratha under Sivaji defied the Moguls in central and southern India and ultimately triumphed over them. The Sikhs rose in the north and set up independent principalities of their own. In the early decades of the 19th century the Mahratha were reduced by the British. In 1849 the last independent Indian kingdom was annexed and the whole of India became a British possession.

The British attitude towards the Hindus and towards the Muslims changed from time to time. For some years after the Mutiny of 1857, in which Muslims had taken a greater part than the Hindus, their policy was distinctly anti-Muslim and pro-Hindu. After the formation of the Indian National Congress in 1885, which began to agitate for freedom and was largely composed of Hindus,

Impassively a stone attendant of Shiva watches pilgrims approach his island temple on Jahangira, sanctified by its site on a bend in the river.

Held up before the shrine on Sagar Island, a child takes his place in the ancient religious cycle which unites 400m lives in his turbulent nation.

their policy became pronouncedly anti-Hindu and pro-Muslim.

The British encouraged Muslim separatism. Under the guise of neutrality they gave Muslims more privileges in services such as the police and the army than their numbers entitled them to. The British encouraged separate educational institutions: Islamic schools and colleges were matched by Hindu and Sikh schools and colleges. In railway stations there were separate restaurants for Hindus and Muslims. Even drinking water booths bore signs – Hindu water, Muslim water.

Hindu-Muslim riots became a normal feature of Indian life. Seldom did a Hindu or Sikh religious procession, passing a mosque, fail to spark a brawl. And every year, at the Muslim festival of *Bakr-id* commemorating Abraham's attempted sacrifice of his son, tension mounted. Muslims made it a point to sacrifice a cow, sacred to Hindus, instead of a ram or a goat. And they took good care to decorate the cow and march it through Hindu streets before taking it to the slaughterhouse.

The British government set the scene for political separatism when it gave Muslims, and later, other religious minorities, separate electorates in elections to legislative bodies. This policy encouraged political parties which represented only the interest of their respective communities. With separate electorates the British gave

43

picture sequence: the Ganges

The world's cargo ships tie up
at Calcutta's Kidderpore docks,
to *Ganga Ma* of less importance
than a pilgrim's tiny offering
in a frail palm leaf boat.

Muslims special privileges and thus kept them from joining the nationalists. Another reason why the Muslims kept aloof from the nationalists was the fact that some of the leading figures in the movement, for instance, Bal Gangadhar Tilak of Maharashtra and Lajpat Rai of the Punjab, were also associated with Hindu revivalism. British patronage and suspicion of Hindu nationalism gave birth to the Muslim League which in 1940 demanded an independent Muslim state, Pakistan.

Although Muslims belong to the same races and speak the same languages as other Indians of the region in which they live, their customs and ways of living differ in some respects. A Muslim child is given a distinctively Muslim name – like Mohammed Ali. Sikhs and Hindus of northern India are often distinguished by having similar names like my own surname for example, Singh. Even Christians in most parts of India retain their Hindu names. A Muslim boy is circumcised and learns verses of the Koran from a Mullah. A Hindu boy has his head shaved and, if he belongs to one of the three upper classes of Hinduism, he wears a sacred thread and is taught Sanskrit texts by a Pandit.

The dietary laws of Hindus and Muslims are different. Hindus worship the cow. The Muslims eat it. Hindus, if not vegetarian, eat pork. Muslims are seldom vegetarian and, like the Jews, consider the pig unclean. Muslims only eat the flesh of an animal slain by being bled to death. Hindus prefer to decapitate their goats. Sikhs go further and consider eating meat of an animal slain in the Muslim fashion to be sinful. There are certain differences in the style of dress of the two peoples. Hindus wear Gandhi caps and *dhotis*. Muslims prefer wearing fezes or caps made of lamb's skin and usually wear loose-fitting pajama trousers. Hindu women wear *saris* and sport a little red dot on their foreheads. Muslim women prefer the Punjabi *salwarkameez* or the baggy *gharara*. Muslim women are often veiled. Hindu women never veil themselves.

Hindus worship a multiplicity of gods, read many sacred texts and venerate innumerable avatars. Muslims worship the one and only Allah, honor Mohammed as his one and only prophet and read the Koran as the only true revelation of God. Hindus go to many places of pilgrimage and wash off their sins in India's many sacred rivers. For the Muslims the only places of pilgrimage are Mecca and Medina, or if they are Shia Muslim, Karbala in Iraq. When a Hindu falls ill he consults a Hindu Vaid learned in the Ayurvedic system of medicine. When a Muslim falls ill he consults a Muslim Hakim, learned in the *Yunani* or Greek system of medicine. When a Hindu dies he is cremated and his ashes immersed in a river or in the ocean. When a Muslim dies he is buried with his face turned towards Mecca.

Muslims look upon Hindus as mean, cunning and cowardly, fit only to be *babus* (clerks) or *banias* (shop-keepers). They dismiss Hindu scholars as sanctimonious gasbags. 'The only language a Hindu understands' say the Muslims 'is the language of the sword.' Hindus look upon the Muslims as dirty, incapable of hard work and grasping. 'Give them one thing and they'll be asking for another' say the Hindus. 'Their mentality is that of the Arab Beduin. They are not the sons of the desert, but its fathers, because wherever they go they create a desert. Look what they did to Hindustan!' In every Indian city there is a Muslim locality distinct from the Hindu area.

The sense of euphoria generated by independence obliterated the differences of race, language and religion. Most people, particularly the young, made a point of describing themselves as Indians and refused to divulge their racial, religious or provincial background. They were proud of being Indian primarily because India was the land of Gandhi and would prove that a people as diverse as themselves could be one nation. There was also a generally shared conviction that in following the path of Gandhi, India would prove to the nations of the world that international disputes could be resolved by honest,

open, peaceful methods instead of by cunning diplomacy or resort to war.

The process of disillusionment began very soon. Hindus and Muslims continued to kill each other. When Gandhi tried to stop them he was assassinated. People said 'We have killed Gandhi but we will keep Gandhism alive.' Even that did not happen. Indian troops invaded and annexed Hyderabad. (Indian politicians called it 'police action'.) Indians fought the Pakistanis in Kashmir. In 1961 India invaded Goa, expelled the Portuguese garrison and annexed all Portuguese occupied territories in India. In 1962 India fought a brief war with China and suffered a humiliating defeat. In 1965 there was another war with Pakistan which ended in a draw. And in 1971 in a third confrontation of arms with Pakistan India gained a decisive victory. These wars with their neighbors made the Indians very conscious of their Indianness but they also realized that by resorting to violence they had proved false to their professions of Gandhism. Gandhism was as dead as Gandhi.

India's internal affairs also started going awry. The population increased at an astonishing rate – from 350 million in 1947 to 541 million in 1971. The pace of development in agriculture and industry was much slower. There were famines in Bihar, Rajasthan, Gujarat and Maharashtra. India had to go begging for food and foreign aid. India continues to be among the poorest and most unlettered countries in the world. Fissiparous tendencies began to re-manifest themselves. Southerners who were Dravidians clamored for a separate Dravidistan. The Sikhs in the north-west agitated for a sovereign Sikh state; the Naga in the north-east for an independent Nagaland. Divisive demands seemed endless and the government set up a National Integration Council.

What then does it mean to be an Indian today? It is to have an exaggerated sense of historical importance as a people who attained an advanced state of civilization before any others; a sanctimonious feeling that we are a spiritual people because we gave the world two important religions, Hinduism and Buddhism, and continue to be more engaged in religious practices than the materialistic west; and a legitimate sense of pride that although we were ruled by a colonial power for 150 years and started our career as an independent nation with many handicaps we have not done too badly.

The expectation of life of an Indian has gone up from 27 years in 1947 to 53 years today; the proportion of literacy from 13 per cent to 33 per cent. Our green revolution has almost made us self-sufficient in food. We are making rapid strides in industry. We are among the leading nations in harnessing atomic energy for industry. We make our own fighter aircraft, automobiles, telephones, bicycles. And above all, we are the world's largest democracy and our people (including women) enjoy a measure of political freedom unknown to any other developing country of the world.

43

Caste

44

Independent India has stripped
his powers — yet earthly
veneration is still accorded
the Maharaja of Jodhpur, of
the second, or 'warrior' caste.

The decline of the Maharajas

From 1947 it has been Indian government policy to reduce not only the effects of caste but also its by-products of class distinctions. The progressively diminished status and circumstances of the maharajas is one outstanding result of this policy. In the remote villages, like the one in Andhra Pradesh described on the following pages the ramifications of the caste system clearly persist.

His Highness Maharaja Sir Ranbir Singh GCIE, KCSI, of Jind (1879-1948) was woken at 4 pm every day by his favorite maharanis massaging his limbs softly and singing in slow melodious tones. He fortified himself for the task of ruling, ordained by caste, God and his British over-lords, by alternately sipping glasses of champagne and cups of tea. His typical day included a protracted bath, prolonged dinner, and at least 25 large pegs of brandy during cards, before he retired to bed with one or more maharanis to seek respite from the rigors of ruling his state. For his exertions he was duly rewarded by his grateful British masters with the highest honors.

Sadly for the maharajas, the withdrawal of the British from India in 1947 removed their major prop. This left two-fifths of India with 100 million people, or a third of the total population, under the jurisdiction of 550 odd, some very odd, princes. They were persuaded to accede to the Indian Union and either received compensation or were guaranteed certain privileges by the Indian Constitution. But in 1972 an Act of Parliament stripped away these privileges, which had included retention of their titles, exemption from customs duties, and payment by the government of an annual allowance called the privy purse.

A postscript may record, however, that if some maharajas were despotic and selfish, others were equally progressive and humane. It was their extravagances that gripped the imagination, and around their portly figures grew such incredible legends of wealth, romance, valor, intrigue and debauchery that they could scarcely all have been fabricated. Poor Maharaja Bhupinder Singh of Patiala (1891-1938) for example, was no weed at 266 lbs., but his endeavors to keep 350 wives and concubines satisfied hastened his end. The 7th Nizam of Hyderabad (1886-1967), believed once to be the richest man in the world, was notoriously careful with his money – even to the extent of smoking the cheapest cigarettes. The maharajas became a social anachronism, a privileged pool of Highnesses among 550 million Lownesses. Their time was up. New social forces, in the person of Mrs Gandhi, swept away the erstwhile princely order. Those who saw the writing on the wall took to politics, business, the diplomatic service or the army, some with great distinction.

The maharajas have disappeared but their legends survive, not so much in their splendid palaces now being converted into luxury hotels, but in common folklore.

45

The priestly Brahman caste is honored most; yet nothing in modern India matched the celebrations of the Prince of Bikaner's splendid wedding.

(Center) The Prince traveled from Bikaner to his wedding in Delhi by silver palanquin, elephant, royal train and white horse.

Caste in a coastal village, Andhra Pradesh

In the village of Aripaka, as in any village in coastal Andhra, the people are grouped into a hierarchy of separate castes or *jati*. The distinctions are social, economic and religious. The divisions and specializations of castes – and their interdependence – form a system which structures all rural life, with variations in different areas. Aripaka, which lies in the sugar cane belt in the region of Anakapalli in the Visakhapatan district, is fairly typical. Most of the castes in the village exist elsewhere throughout coastal Andhra, although the principal farming caste, the Gavara, is found only in this district. Nevertheless the Gavara's position closely parallels that of the Reddi, Kamma, Kapu and Velama which are prominent farming castes in other parts of coastal Andhra.

The castes are traditionally ranked in hierarchical order. There are the three *varna,* or religious categories of Twice-born castes (so called after their ritual rebirth ceremony) who are made up of priests, warriors and merchants. There are the Shudra castes, the fourth *varna* or religious category, of farmers and laborers. And the Harijan, formerly called outcastes or untouchables, who are outside the *varna*. The position of the castes in Aripaka in this traditional ritual hierarchy corresponds broadly, but not precisely, with their economic functions. There is no simple one-for-one relationship of caste status and economic status. The traditional landlords, who are members of the highest or Twice-born castes, have declined in wealth and importance since the 1950s. Simultaneously the farmers, who are only Shudra, but in many ways the core of the settlement, have risen in importance as the largest landowning group and the principal source of employment and income for most of the other castes. As 46 per cent of the total village population, the largest single caste, they dominate Aripaka economically and politically. Although they are the major landowning group in the village, individual holdings are usually not large. Most families farm and work their own land; however a few families with large holdings employ fulltime field laborers who are paid annually in kind. Although the farmers' ritual status as Shudra is not high – they are preceded by two castes, Jangam and Wadram, with priestly functions – it is not very low. Those others with whom they share the Shudra caste, most of the specialized service or laborer castes, are lower than the farmers. Members of the service castes depend on the farmers for their living. Often they are attached for long periods to families of the farmer caste and are paid yearly for their services in grain or cash. This arrangement, which is characteristic of villages in many regions of India, is often called the *jajmati* system. Although some economically depressed Shudra service castes who do not follow their traditional service occupation work for the farmers as laborers, most landless laborers come from the Harijan castes which are the lowest in status.

Modern politics cuts across caste barriers: in India's parliament to represent his state, the Maharaja of Gwalior meets untouchables.

(Right) Among the old rulers like the Maharaja of Udaipur standing atop his Lake Palace (the model for the Taj Mahal) 'class' has superseded 'caste'.

Caste

Caste evolved to give society
cohesion, not division. Many
trade castes combined to build
the Nagarjunasagar dam
across the Krishna river.

Outside the hierarchy of Hindu life, a gypsy woman, identified by the solid silver 'earrings' suspended from her hair, can choose her own role.

The Hindu has an intense identification with nature. All creatures 'are produced by food, live by food, and pass back into food'.

The Gavara trap water in reservoirs during the monsoon. They use the large areas that cannot be irrigated to raise millet and vegetables. On irrigated land they grow rice and the principal cash crop, sugar cane. The sugar cane is crushed and boiled down into a crude sugar called jaggery, which the farmers sell in the market in Anakapalli, 15 miles away. They deal mainly with Gavara merchants who originally learnt the trade working as weighboys for the Komati merchants (the third Twice-born, merchant caste) and gradually took over, and now have an equal say with the Komati in running the Anakapalli jaggery market.

As befits their central economic position, Gavara now hold the traditional post of hereditary headman (*munsif*) as well as the new elective posts of *panchayat* president and vice-president. Although castes generally solve internal disputes on their own, where they do not the Gavara head the hierarchy for settling disputes for the service and landless laborer castes.

It is the Gavara who most prominently patronize the celebration of the village goddess festivals. Some Gavara surname groups have special relationships and obligations to particular goddesses. At the festivals Gavara are frequently seen performing dances, displays of stick twirling and mythological dramas. On one level these festivals are intended to pacify the goddess with animal sacrifice, and prevent her from letting loose epidemics in the village. On another level they reaffirm social unity and cooperation between all the village's caste groups.

In Aripaka the Brahman caste who belong to the highest Twice-born caste, the first of the three *varna* categories, have the highest status in the village. Theirs is a small caste which owns some land that it allows farmers and landless laborers to cultivate in return for half the crop yield. The Brahman sub-group, Pradhama Saka Niyogi, is prohibited in Aripaka from performing rituals for others and has traditionally specialized in government service. Members of this caste remain fairly unobtrusive in the life of the village, except for the village record keeper, the *karanam*. The *karanam*, as well as helping the Gavara *munsif* to collect taxes and maintain law and order, is the local authority on the astrological almanac which the villagers consult for auspicious times to begin planting, harvesting, house building, weddings, and many other domestic rituals.

The Brahman priests, who perform domestic rituals, come to Aripaka from nearby villages. Different priests specialize in the often very different rituals of particular castes: they name children, celebrate weddings, propitiate family ancestors, celebrate the beginning of a child's studies, or the entering of a new house. When a child is born or a girl starts menstruating at an inauspicious time a priest will appease malevolent astrological influences, hold a Satyanarayana Vratam – a thanksgiving and well-being ceremony in praise of the god Vishnu – or officiate at the investiture of Twice-born caste males with the 49

However small his 'farm' a landowner's caste forbids him manual work – though he may starve, he employs a laborer to work his land.

(Bottom) This Mala boy is 'untouchable' *(Harijan)*. He may not 'defile' the village well. Some *Harijan* tie a brush behind to remove footmarks.

sacred thread. For these services, and for chanting the appropriate Sanskrit prayers, the Brahman is given a small sum of money and some uncooked food used in the ceremony – such as rice, vegetables, fruit and coconuts.

The Raju caste, classified as the Kshatriya or warriors among the Twice-born castes, is the second highest in the village. The Raju are descendants of former rulers of the area and though their wealth and influence has declined they still bestow patronage in the form of land, money and political connections. Several Raju families have Shudra and Harijan field laborers attached to them by yearly agreements. In return the Raju offer daily meals, cigars, clothes and a yearly quota of grain. Raju, like the other two Twice-born castes, are highly educated. In Aripaka the doctor and a schoolteacher are Raju.

The third Twice-born caste in Aripaka is the Komati caste, also sometimes called by their Sanskrit name *vaisya,* meaning merchants. Most of the Komati are small traders who sell the villagers grain, spices, tea, cooking oil, kerosene, tobacco, and items for rituals such as incense, camphor and colored powders. In the early 1950s the Komati were the largest landowners of the village and lived in luxury. But a series of financial failures combined with the growing wealth of the Gavara farmers, who had earned money as migrant laborers in Burma, set the Komati into a decline from which they have never fully recovered. Several Komati families still own land which they give out for sharecropping, but their main source of income is their small shops.

The Gavara's money and surplus food goes back into the village economy in the form of payments to service castes. These Shudra and Harijan service castes perform important functions in the domestic rituals of their patrons as well as in the village festivals. They also perform rituals linked with their occupations or crafts during Sankranti, a harvest festival in January when ancestors are worshipped and chickens sacrificed to the tools of their various trades. Of all these service castes carpenters, barbers and washermen stand out as having particularly stable relations with their patrons, receiving annual payments in grain or cash.

The Kamsali, the village carpenters and blacksmiths, are very important to the farmer. They make his plows, sickles, bullock carts, vats for preparing jaggery, house beams, door frames, beds and many other farming and domestic utensils. Several Kamsali families are gold-smiths and make much of the villagers' jewelry. Kamsali also have the duty of carving two wooden idols, the focus of the festival procession to the village goddesses' temple. There are twelve Kamsali families in Aripaka, which are usually attached to Gavara, though many also work for the Brahman, Raju, Komati, Kapu and Velama – minority farmer castes similar to the Gavara – and a few toddy tappers – traditional toddy farmers – who own land. Odd jobs for other people are done strictly for cash.

The Mangali, the village barbers, are similarly linked,

Caste members refuse to accept food from people of lower status, but here barber and Mala women grind corn for a Gowra farmer's wife.

Kamsali blacksmiths and carpenters are vital to the farmers. Their castes make his tools and carve wooden idols of village goddesses.

not only to most Gavara households, but also to some Twice-born caste families. Members of other service castes or landless laborers merely pay for each haircut or shave. Barbers usually serve about thirty-eight patron families throughout the year. There are only four barbers in Aripaka, but they play important roles in many rituals: they perform a child's first haircutting ceremony, and at weddings they ceremonially cut the bride's and groom's nails and bathe them. At festivals they shave the heads of villagers who have vowed to give their hair to the village goddess or to a local Shiva temple. Barbers are also drummers at weddings, at processions for Gairamma (a harvest festival in honor of Shiva's consort Gauri) and at processions to the temple of the village goddess, in which they also carry her palm-leaf umbrella.

The ten Tsakali caste washermen families in Aripaka are attached to about thirty patron families who pay them annually in grain for washing and pressing their clothes. Washermen serve a wider variety of castes on an annual basis than either the carpenters or the barbers. They have many ritual duties. At Gavara weddings they carry the bride and groom around the village in a palanquin. At the weddings of most other castes they receive a ceremonial payment and carry the bride's dowry of brass. When a patron's daughter first menstruates the washerman is given all her old clothes. He also

Caste

Barbers play important ritual roles: ceremonial bathing and nail-cutting at weddings, a child's first hair-cutting ceremony, festival drumming.

(Bottom) Barbers sacrifice a cock to their tool boxes during *Sankranti* after the harvest when Shudra and Harijan castes also worship their ancestors.

Washermen are given annual payments of grain by their patron families. Some also send their women begging for left-over food in the evening.

At a ceremony propitiating his ancestors a Gowra washes the feet of a Brahman priest. Touching feet implies great deference and respect.

receives money and cloth for taking part in funeral rituals and tending pyres for other castes. In the festival of the village goddess it is a washerman who traditionally carries a torch and it has recently become customary for a particular washerman to become possessed by the goddess, who expresses her satisfaction or displeasure with the proceedings through him.

The other service castes in the village – the Jangam, the village tailors who also serve as priests to most of the Shudra castes – oilpressers (Telukua), the village goddess priest (Wadram), the toddy tappers (Yata or Settigollu), and the weavers (Padmasali) – do not have long-term relationships with particular families, perhaps because they perform services required less regularly. They are, however, important in one way or another in the economic and ritual life of the village. The Jangam, the village tailor, is the priest in the village temple of the god Rama and the Jangam's special drum is required at weddings and ritual processions. They are most needed however for a Shaivite funeral ritual (using a bell and conch-shell horn) performed for the Shudra castes.

The oilpressers press the sesame and groundnut grown by the farmers at one of the two bullock-run oilpresses which serve the needs of the village. They perform their service for cash or a share of the oil, and do not perform any special ritual functions for any other caste.

The village goddess priest and his family, on the other hand, seem only to have the purely ritual function of supervising rituals in honor of the village goddess. They are the custodians of the *ghattam* pots which are used to collect offerings to the goddess. The priest himself occasionally becomes possessed by the goddess at her festival. For most of the year he depends on wages for working in the farmers' fields and on what he can raise on his own small plot of land.

Following the prohibition of their traditional occupation and their migration to Burma in the 1930s, the toddy tappers have completely given up taking sap from the palmyra palm which they would ferment into an intoxicating drink. Though some toddy tappers in the region are now licensed to make a liquor from sugar cane, the toddy tappers of Aripaka mainly depend for a living on selling firewood gathered in the nearby hills, making mats and palm-leaf containers, and working as farm laborers. Their ritual duty is to carry a goddess's brass horses out to her temple in one of the festival processions.

The Harijan castes, the landless laborers without any particular specialized craft, include the Mala and the Madiga. The Mala depend on the farmers for employment as field hands and a number of them are attached for long periods to farmer families by the *jajmati* system and are paid annually in grain or cash. One Mala is the Barki, the hereditary servant of the village headman and the village record keeper. Every ritual procession and wedding has a Mala drummer, and the Barki has a particularly prominent role in the village goddess

festivals. The Madiga remove farmers' dead cattle, tan the hides to sell or to make drums, and dry the meat. One Madiga is the sweeper of the village streets and Madiga drummers are indispensable at processions and as town-criers.

Apart from their economic relationship with each other all the castes have customs that distinguish them and indicate their rank. Each caste usually lives in a distinct quarter of the village. Friendships tend to be formed within the caste, or between people who are equally rich or poor. Wedding rituals, despite overall similarities, are peculiar to each caste. Regulations on marriage differ from caste to caste. The twice-born castes and the carpenters (who claim to have been Brahman before the present Brahman displaced them) strictly prohibit divorce or the remarriage of widows. But these are both quite common practices among many Shudra and Harijan castes. Twice-born castes and carpenters restrict their women's activities but most Shudra and Harijan women play important economic roles. Gavara women sell produce in the local markets, and women of the laborer caste frequently work in the fields.

Dress is another way in which status is sometimes expressed. The men of the three Twice-born castes – Brahman, Raju and Komati – and the carpenters are the only people who wear the sacred thread received in a ceremony signifying spiritual rebirth, the origin of the term Twice-born. Carpenters, Shudra and Harijan wear scanty loincloths when at work. Women of certain castes have, although increasingly rarely, distinctive jewelry which signifies their caste. Older Gavara women may still wear strands of large coral beads and a unique type of silver bangle. Velama women have distinctive earrings, nose ornaments and hairstyles.

A member of one caste will refuse boiled food prepared by a caste considered inferior to his own. He will, however, accept such food if it is prepared by a caste considered superior in status to his own. Brahman refuse to accept food from any other caste. Raju accept it only from Brahman. Komati, in spite of being considered lower than Raju, will only accept food from Brahman because they are vegetarians. The Gavara accept food from all the Twice-born castes as well as the priestly Jangam and Wadram castes. Oilpressers accept it from Gavara and all those from whom the Gavara accept. The barbers and washermen accept food from all Twice-born castes and all Shudra, except the toddy tappers. Neither of them will accept food from each other however. The toddy tappers accept food from all Twice-born and Shudra castes in the village. The Mala and Madiga Harijan castes accept food from all Twice-born castes and Shudra, but refuse to accept food from each other. The carpenters are somewhat exceptional in that they, like the Brahman, refuse to accept food from any other caste but differ from the Brahman, however, in that no other caste will accept food from them.

53

Parsees Bombay

On Bombay's Malabar Hill stand four round, massive structures built entirely of stone. Above them circle large flocks of vultures, for it is to the *Dokhmas*, or Towers of Silence, that the Parsee dead are brought to be devoured by birds. The wealthy inhabitants of Malabar Hill occasionally grumble about the vultures but have become resigned to sharing with them this exclusive section of Bombay. Though most non-Parsees in India might not appreciate this method of disposing of the dead, they do have considerable respect for the Parsees. The Parsee community has been able to exert decisive influence upon public life in Bombay where about 70 per cent of its 100,600 members live. During the last two centuries the Parsees in India have come to play a noteworthy role in the domain of economics, politics, science and the arts which is out of proportion to their negligibly small number.

The Parsees have not always had such a prestigious position in India. The word 'Parsee' is a derivation of *Pars,* now known as *Fars,* one of the provinces of ancient Persia. For over a thousand years there was no record of them in the western world and European scholars believed that the Persian culture, above all the ancient religion of Zarathustra or Zoroastrianism, had ceased to exist. But a small band of Persians held tenaciously to their beliefs, withstood conversion to Islam and fled over the Arabian Sea to India. They first landed at Diu in Kathiawar then later moved to Sanjan on the coast of Gujarat in 785.

A traditional story of the Parsees relates that when they arrived at Sunjan the Hindu king Jadi Rana sent one of his servants bearing a jug brim-full of milk to indicate that there was no room for them. One of the Parsees slid a coin into the milk without spilling a drop and sent the jug back to the king. They settled in Sanjan. They became small traders and farmers under the Hindu rulers. Although they donned Indian clothes and Gujarati became their mother-tongue, the Parsees refused to admit new converts to Parsism or to marry outside.

In 1490 Sanjan was conquered by the Muslims and the Parsees again fled south to settle in the coastal region between Surat and present-day Bombay. There they resumed their occupations of trading and farming until the arrival of the European trading companies in India. The Europeans began using the services of the Parsees as mediators, interpreters and trading agents, roles for which the Parsees were especially suited. Drawn by the wealth and social prestige gained by these functions, the Parsees rapidly moved to the trading centers of western India, first to Broach and Surat but, since the beginning of the 18th century, increasingly to Bombay.

The Parsees have always been equally devoted to philanthropic enterprise. Today the Parsee *panchayat* (council) in Bombay administers over a thousand foundations. The Parsee community is exceptional for it can justifiably claim that no beggars can be found among

54

(Top) By Zoroastrianism, their ancient Persian faith, the Parsees believe a man achieves salvation through purity of thought, word and action.

A Parsee child is invested with the sacred shirt, *sudrah*, and sacred thread, *kusti*, at the age of seven at the *naojote* ceremony.

The girl's grandmother watches the *naojote* ceremony. Her parents and family now have a sacred responsibility to give her a good moral education.

any of its members. There are very few communities in India that can say the same. Parsee riches are not corrupting: they are connected with the Zoroastrian responsibility to help the needy to the glory of God'.

One explanation for the Parsees' extra-communal philanthropy can be seen in the occupational structure of the community. In comparison to other Indian communities there has been a very high percentage of Parsees in professional occupations and an infinitesimally small number in jobs which cannot provide financial security. Of the 49,000 Parsees living in Bombay in the middle of the 19th century almost half were priests, 34 per cent were contractors, 21 per cent were distillers, 19 per cent were watchmakers, 19 per cent were accountants, 17 per cent were bankers, salesmen and moneylenders, and 13 per cent each were teachers and lawyers. As is evident from the above figures, many Parsees engaged in more than one occupation. Less than 1 per cent of the community pursued the lower occupations – unskilled labor, fishing, portering and musical entertainment. And there were no Parsees among Bombay's numerous and impoverished washermen, smiths, butchers, weavers, scavengers and beggars. Today the Anglicized surnames such as Engineer, Readymoney, Doctor, Printer, Paymaster, Bonesetter, Sodawater-bottlewalla recall the Parsee bias for upper and middle class occupations.

Unlike other Indian communities, the Parsees had no taboos against acquiring British-European customs. A 55

Parsees Bombay

To keep the elements undefiled,
Parsee dead are taken to the
Towers of Silence where they
are placed in the central well
and devoured by vultures.

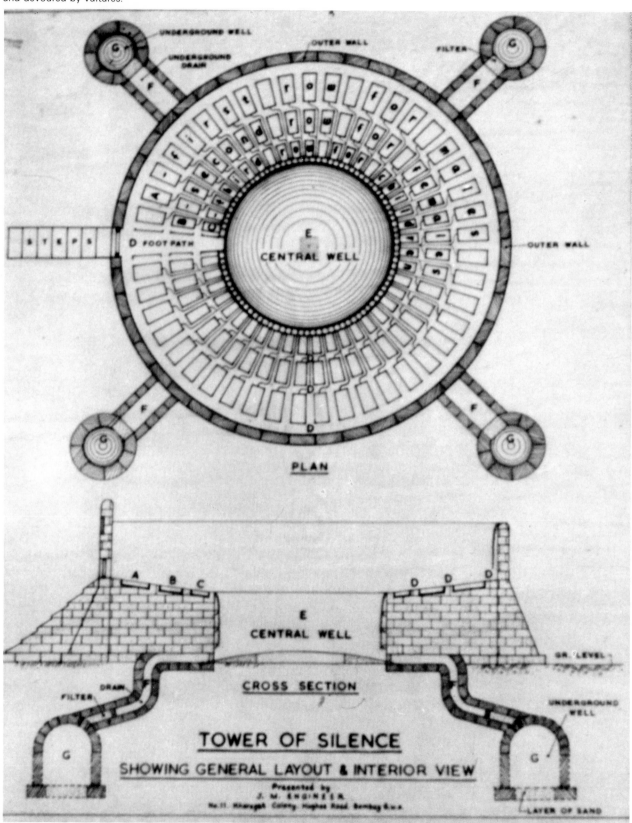

PLAN

CROSS SECTION

TOWER OF SILENCE

SHOWING GENERAL LAYOUT & INTERIOR VIEW

Presented by
J. M. ENGINEER.

Two white-clad bearers of
the dead take rich and poor
alike to the *Dokhmas,* Towers
of Silence, for all men
are united in death.

Parsee gentleman would consider himself to be a relative
of the Europeans and often spoke disparagingly of the
Indian 'natives'. He played cricket, read English novels,
drank Scotch and soda and imported his furniture from
Europe. If he was very wealthy he would have his
daughters educated by an English governess and send
his sons away for schooling in England. But while the
men still wear western clothes, many of the women now
prefer the Indian sari to European dresses. The more
traditional men wear a dark-colored rimless cap that
must never be removed in the presence of an equal.

Beneath the garments of a Parsee man or woman is
worn the *kusti,* or sacred thread, woven from lambs' wool
into seventy-two threads, divided into six strands. Three
tassels, each of fourteen threads, are formed at the end
of each woven thread. The *kusti* is worn around the waist
over a shirt of white cambric called a *sudreh.* The *sudreh*
and *kusti* are presented to a Parsee child in his seventh
year at an initiation ceremony or *navjote.* The *sudreh* and
kusti are emblems of purity and innocence given to
remind a child of the purity of life which he has always
to observe. As the *kusti* is tied to the initiate, where it will
remain throughout his life, he recites the last and most
important part of the Articles of Faith: 'Oh, Almighty!
Come to my help. I am a Zoroastrian worshipper of God.
I agree to praise the Zoroastrian religion, and to believe

in it. I praise good thoughts, good words and good deeds.'

Beyond these three fundamental rules, a good Zoroastrian must embrace truth, justice, loyalty, purity,
diligence, peaceableness and charity. The life-affirming
Zoroastrian ethics do not permit asceticism in any form,
and injurious animals such as vermin and snakes are to
be destroyed as the embodiment of evil. The contrast to
Hinduism and Buddhism is clear in these principles.

To maintain air, water, earth and fire pure and undefiled is a cardinal principle of the Zoroastrian creed.
These elements are creations of the Almighty and as
such are to be respected by man. (Fire has a significant
symbolical role in Zoroastrian ritual and consequently it
earned the Zoroastrians the misnomer 'fire-worshippers'.)
All that is dead is considered to be impure and should
be disposed of in such a manner as not to defile the four
elements or injure the living. That is why the Parsees do
not bury or burn their dead, or consign them to water.
Instead, they leave the bodies on platforms inside high
wells, where the bones are picked clean by vultures and
then are pulled by gravity into a mixture of lime and
phosphorus where they eventually disintegrate. Rich
and poor alike are brought to these Towers of Silence,
for all men are united at death. By surrendering one's
body to the birds to prevent pollution of the elements,
the Parsee performs his final act of charity.

57

Monsoon and the life cycle

For three months before the
monsoon arrives nearly 600
million Indians suffer an
intense heat, sleeping,
waiting for life-giving rain.

The people of India, who are subject to the monsoon, have learnt to take the calamities – the famines, the floods and the cyclones – as they come. They do not add to their worries by thinking about them in advance. Indeed they have got into the habit of forgetting about the calamities, much as the people of Japan, Peru and California are forgetful of their earthquakes.

The scale of death and destruction varies according to the disaster. The greatest number of deaths happen when prolonged and widespread drought brings about famine. Among the worst in the last two hundred years were in Bengal in 1769-70 when deaths were estimated at anything from one-tenth to one-third of the population; all over India in 1876-78 when five million died; again all over India in 1896-97 with a similar number of deaths; and in 1899-1900 when over three million died.

The outside world hears about the monsoon only when it is abnormal – when it is either absent or over-abundant. Reports of famines, floods and cyclones move people not only to read about them but also to act, and they send substantial relief for the victims. The monsoon in India has become a matter of international concern. Deaths from famine can be reduced these days by rushing in food from outside. The shocking loss of life and suffering which resulted from two recent famines in Bengal in 1943-44 and in Bihar in 1966-67, were due more to negligence than to the famines themselves.

Famines create scenes of death which are ghastly and squalid. They can never evoke the sense of awe that other spectacles of man's pitiful helplessness against the destructive forces of nature always do. In spite of being calamitous, cyclones, storm surges and floods have a tragic grandeur. It is the storm surges in the coastal regions which send banks of water ten to fifteen feet high rushing inland for many miles with terrible force that cause death in the largest numbers. Some cyclones are only a little less destructive. The floods on the other hand destroy crops and cattle but are less dangerous to life.

I have seen what cyclones and floods can do. In September 1919 a great cyclone, about 50 miles wide, swept up from the Bay of Bengal to the Garo Hills littering the districts of Barisal, Faridpur, Dacca and Mymensingh with wreckage. The depth to which it spiraled inland was something like 250 miles. Next day I was traveling from Calcutta to my birthplace in Mymensingh. Aboard a steamer on the Brahmaputra river I noticed that the trees on the eastern bank looked battered and torn. It must have been a severe storm, I thought. It was after reaching Mymensingh town that I learned what had really happened. We were told that the train for my town might not go, for the telegraph lines had been brought down and there was no communication between the stations. Towards dusk the train started. After a few miles I saw a number of goods wagons lying on their sides in a rice field. They had been blown some distance away from the track.

Monsoon and the life cycle

Hoping to catch the slightest breeze a farmer stretches out on his *charpoy*. He cannot work his rock-hard field until the rain brings it to life again.

(Right) Sometimes the cycle fails and famine comes instead of rain. Children and old people die first, their skins as parched as the earth.

It was at midnight that I reached my town, and finding no carriage decided to walk home – a distance of about two miles. It was pitch dark and, what was worse, the road was blocked every few hundred yards with fallen trees. In places they were piled so high that I had to climb down to the dry river bed and skirt them. The next morning I saw what had happened to the town. Except for its few brick houses which withstood the cyclone it was a tumble-down place. I saw big corrugated iron roofs from the magistrates' bungalows lying in the fields. They had been blown away like kites.

I also learned how it had come and how it had raged. From midnight people had seen a tawny glare in a sky which was solidly overcast. Then a noise, as of many thousands of bass drums, was heard and grew louder and louder. At three in the morning the cyclone struck the town and went on for about three hours. After that there was a lull before the cyclone returned, according to its anti-clockwise spiraling motion, from the opposite side. It continued for another three hours. A few days later I went to my ancestral village and found our big homestead almost wholly wrecked. The loss of life was also appalling. In the city of Dacca alone thousands were drowned in the Buriganga river.

The flood which I saw was the one in north Bengal in 1922. I was coming to Calcutta in the train from Sirajganj. In Bengal, as it happens, all the railway lines run across the natural slope of the drainage basins. So this line blocked a number of rivers and slowed down the passage of the flood waters. It was a brilliant moonlit night and I could see sheets of water gleaming like silver. Only under the bridges I saw foaming cataracts of water. I also saw an extraordinary exception to the law that water finds its own level. The flood had come up to the height of the track on the upstream side and was about six feet lower on the other. On the tracks, refugee jackals were sitting without paying any heed to the train and its noise. They were sitting on their haunches, muzzles upturned to the sky, and howling at the moon for this monstrous reversal of the order of nature. When I came to Calcutta I saw that the many colonies of the prostitutes of the great city had become daytime street-walkers on a mission of mercy. They went through the streets in processions, singing songs of appeal composed for the occasion. Looking at one of the parties in front of my office, I could see no allure in their expression or their clothes or their singing. I thought the crystalline waters I had seen the previous night had washed away their sin, to make them fit to pose as *petite* Mary Magdalenes. Even an English colonel watched them with interest from a window and sent them some money.

But it is necessary to see these calamities for what they really are in the lives of those who suffer from them. Death is always shocking in its immediate impact, but it is also quickly and easily forgotten, which is as well, because all men are under a sentence of death with only

The Indian climate rules the people with its unending cycle of death and dramatic regeneration. An old man waits through the last hot month.

indefinite reprieve. The destruction brought about more tangible losses, but these too were quickly made up. In the west homelessness is a terrifying notion, for it brings to the mind the sense of desolation which certainly prompted Jesus to say: 'Foxes have holes, and birds of the air have nests; but the son of man hath nowhere to lay his head.'

In India people live under half-shelter as they do in half-starvation. The houses are flimsy and if they tumble down easily they are also easily re-erected. For centuries my ancestors were well-to-do people. Yet up to my twelfth year I lived in huts built with bamboo, wood, thatch, mats and corrugated iron, standing on mud platforms, and at dawn or when the moon was full I could see the light twinkling like stars through minute holes.

In the monsoon lands of the true tropics, in East Bengal, Assam, Burma or Malaya, human habitations are only transformed vegetation, and therefore I call their way of life 'living in the bamboo economy'. But in upper India, all over the plain of the Ganges, people live in the 'mud economy' of the Middle East, in huts made of sun-baked clay. In the vast plain the dividing line between the mud and bamboo economies can be drawn around longitude 88° east. West of this line the early colonizers of India, who came from the middle east, did not properly adapt their way of life to the monsoon, and suffered as a consequence. Water does more harm to mud than to grass. Still, even mud dries as quickly under sun as it melts under rain. After the cyclones I have spoken of all the huts demolished by it were rebuilt in about six weeks.

Over the whole of East Bengal man becomes amphibious in the rainy season. In many districts, during these months, people have to use rafts to go visiting or shopping, and even to go from the kitchen which is in one hut to the bedroom which is in another. In years of very heavy rains the hut floors remain under water. My mother told me that once, when she was taken by her mother to her uncle's village in a low-lying area, she could see water snakes swimming all around her bed.

For miles, in places for twenty or thirty miles, fields under cultivation became vast lakes. Passing through one of them I once saw that the boatmen could not hit the bottom with their fifteen-foot punting poles. But, in other seasons, paddy was grown in them and in the cold weather people walked through them. Near my ancestral village I have walked through rice fields during the cold season and then from boats, in the rainy season, seen them sown with water lily.

It is only in those areas which are close to the hills, and through which rivers with shallow beds flow to the great draining rivers, that great damage is done by spates and sudden floods. This is because of the speed at which the water level rises. But these waters also recede within weeks. The flooded areas of easternmost Bengal remain under water for several months.

62

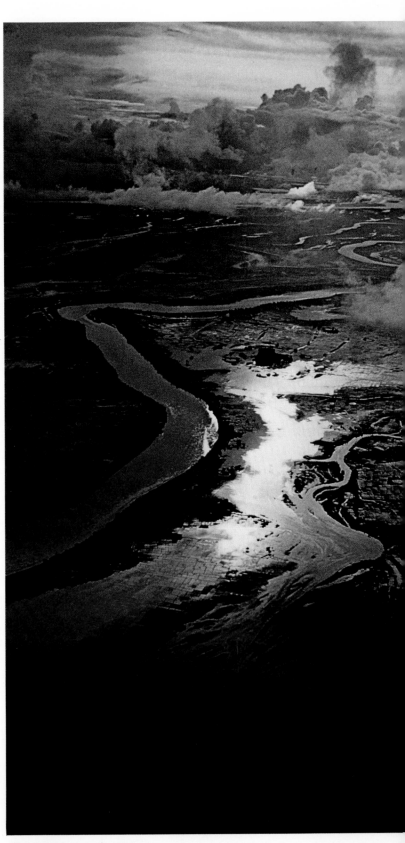

The clouds' wrote the poet Kalidasa, 'come forward as kings among tumultuous armies; their flags are the lightning, the thunder is their drum.

In the west it is spring. In India the monsoon season is the time when lovers prepare to meet, like the lady in a 17th century Rajput miniature.

The people of India have learnt to live with the sorrows that their environment lays on them. There is no escape because the environment can indefinitely defy any fussy bureaucratic meddling with it. Nature, in India, will permit no interference. So the people of India take their natural calamities as being all in the day's work; for the rest, they find happiness in the good that the monsoon brings. They would no more question nature's fury than they would God's wrath. Actually, all phenomena of nature have a double aspect – overwhelmingly benevolent, but also occasionally destructive and there is beauty in both.

In the vast region from Assam to the Punjab the monsoon has a close relationship with the river system which carries away its precipitation to the sea. While the rain-bearing clouds sweep north-westwards the water flows in exactly the opposite direction. Between them the monsoon and the rivers maintain the cyclical movement of water – from the sea to the sky, from the sky to the earth, and from earth back again to the sea. For miles the Ganges and its tributaries carry the immense precipitation on the slopes of the Himalayas, the Vindhyas and on the plain itself in a single broad channel. After reaching Bengal the great river divides into braids like the Nile below Cairo, and flows into the sea through a number of channels. Even so the discharge of water by the westernmost channel, the Hooghly, was such (before its junction with the main channel was silted up) that in the days of sail, approaching ships were slowed down 50 miles before reaching the mouth of the estuary. As Bishop Heber wrote, at the end of his voyage to Calcutta, the mighty Ganges was running like a mill-stream a fathom or two beneath the surface, and nothing but a powerful gale could help ships against it. That was in 1823.

As if that was not enough, after reaching the heart of Bengal's alluvial plain, the main stream of the Ganges (known as the Padma) was joined by two other great rivers which carried still more water between them than the Ganges. The first of these was the Brahmaputra which brought down water not only from Tibet but also from Assam valley, an area of heavy rainfall. The second river was the Meghna, which carried all the water from a catchment area of the heaviest rainfall in the world. In one place, Cherrapunji, the annual rainfall is 428 inches. A semicircle of ranges formed by the Garo Hills, Naga Hills, Cachar Hills, Lushai Hills and Chittagong Hills block the monsoon on three sides, and that results in rains which convert the district of Sylhet into one vast lake studded with village islets on high ground. All this water first flows down two rivers, the Kalni and the Bibiyana, and after that down the Meghna which is a combination of the former rivers. It is the deepest and darkest water course I have seen, and it joins the Padma below Dacca, to form a broad and dangerous estuary in which high bores are common.

This great river system covering the whole of north

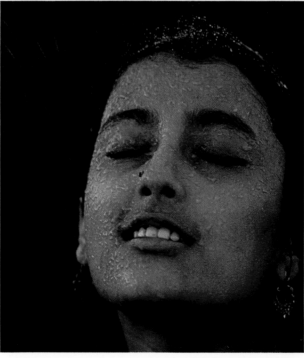

At last the first rains break – drenching the whole world in a glorious splashing downpour. The people come alive again.

Monsoon and the life cycle

The lowering clouds burst apart and a banana seller in Bombay flings on a plastic coat and dashes through the streets for cover.

India from Assam to the Punjab constitutes a colossal hydrographic system, of which the atmospheric water brought in by the monsoon must be regarded as a part. They create one complete ambiance for human life by working together. Without the rivers the great plain would revert to its original condition of an inland sea. Without the monsoon it would become a desert. But between them they sustain a population which is among the densest of any agricultural region in the world.

It is natural that a people whose existence depends on the monsoon should have an emotional fervor about it. This has been expressed since the earliest times of literate Indian people. Sanskrit literature contains beautiful descriptions of the rainy season. The early epic Ramayana describes the season in a whole canto, the 28th of the fourth book. Rama has had to postpone his expedition to rescue his wife Sita on account of the rains, and is waiting impatiently on a south Indian hill. But he cannot help noticing the scene before his eyes, and he describes it to his brother. I quote Griffith's translation of the Sanskrit verses:

'See, brother, see,' thus Rama cried
On Malyavat's dark-wooded side,
'A chain of clouds, like lofty hills,
The sky with gathering shadow fills,
Nine months those clouds have borne the load

The Ganges flows strongly now and joy turns to fear. People pray for the rain to stop before floods sweep everything away.

A single sheet of rain falls
from the sky and villagers
press themselves against walls
seeking the meager protection
of overhanging eaves.

Conceived from sunbeams as they glowed,
And, having drunk the seas, give birth,
And drop their offspring on the earth.'

He goes on to say that at daytime the clouds wreath
the sun like garlands, and at sunset the sun makes their
fringes fiery red:

And the winds in their caverns moan
Sound like the voice's undertone.
From east to west red lightning's flash,
And, quivering 'neath the golden lash,
The great sky like a generous steed
Groans inly at each call to speed.

So the description goes on for 67 couplets. A great
Sanskrit poem of the classical age describes the upper
reaches of the Godavari river in these words: 'Here are
the Prasravana Hills, with their soft blue made softer still
by the ever-drizzling clouds, their caverns echoing the
babbling Godavari, their woods a solid mass of azure,
made up of tangled foliage.'

And the most famous poem about the rains in Sanskrit
is the *Meghaduta* by Kalidasa. It tells of a *yaksha*, a sort
of demigod, who has been exiled by his king and is
spending his exile on a hill in central India. He sees the
first clouds appear and implores them as they go north
to carry a message of love to his wife beyond the
Himalayas. Every stage of the passage of the clouds is
described, until they strike the mountain in billowy
terraces to form an opalescent stairway to the abode of
Shiva and Parvati.

We always see the coming of the rains as Wordsworth
saw the rainbow, and if we could not we would certainly
say like him: 'Or let me die'. On the plain of the Ganges
their coming is not simply a phase in the cycle of the
seasons; in their sudden and heavy onset they bring
about a revolution. Even the spring in northern countries
does not give such an impression of change. In Bengal
the coming of rain makes us pass from one state of happiness to another, for there the summer too has a lifegiving
quality: it ripens not only the mango, jack-fruit and
melon, but also the earth, which becomes seasoned and
mellowed. Summer's sound-effect is the incessant chirp-
ing of the crickets at noontide. But in less than a week
the rains change the scene. The sky becomes grave and
sad, and at times sends down liquid crystal, at others
opaline drizzle. During the day the clouds vary in their
color from the deepest collyrium blue to soft pearly
shades, and at night the moon lines the beautiful cirro-
cumulus clouds with amber. The ceaseless treble of the
crickets gives place to croaking of the frogs in their
thousands, which sound as if they are playing only two
bass notes on an enormous organ by day and night.

But the coming of the rains in upper India is like the
arrival of a relieving force to a besieged city in its last
gasps. After three months of torture from heat, winds,
dust when nothing feels cool to the touch even in the
early morning, men begin to feel as if they would go mad.

65

(Over page) Worshippers
splash up to the hilltop temple
at Jagannath in thanksgiving
to Shiva, the creator and —
like rain — giver of life.

Monsoon and the life cycle

The earth is flooded and 30,000 people can be made homeless in a night. A tributary of the Mahanadi floods part of Orissa.

(Bottom) Mud homes swept away by floods are easily rebuilt. A bag of rice has been saved. When the waters recede life can begin again.

A farmer leads his oxen through his kingdom, magically transformed by six weeks of rain from parched earth into vivid green paddy fields.

All life is revered by Hindus, and together, the whole of creation joins in the celebration of moisture and the new life it brings.

Kipling wrote that what could be seen then was neither sky, sun nor horizon – nothing but a purple haze of heat. It was as though the earth was dying of apoplexy. The monsoon is welcomed, like a relief force. I felt like this after my first summer in Delhi.

There is also a difference in the feeling about the rains between Bengal and upper India. In Bengal the season is the time for keeping indoors unless one is compelled to go out on business, as the winter is in England. In northern India, in contrast, this is the time for picnics and outings, for the clouds create shade. During the rains I see Muslim women, dressed in all-enveloping *burqua*, come out of their homes and roam about in the parks. Babur, the first Mogul emperor of India, also noted that the rains were very pleasant in India, which otherwise he thought had no natural beauty.

It was impossible that a phenomenon which was so vital to human existence in India should not have made an impact on the religion of her people. So it did in fact. Many of the earliest beliefs, prayers and rites of the Hindus are connected with rain. A large number of the hymns of the Rig-Veda, the earliest scripture of the Hindus, are prayers to Indra and other gods for rain. The fire sacrifices, which are so important a feature of the Vedic religion, were also performed to bring rain. Rain was thought the gift of the gods and could not be expected unless the gods were given their due. Here is part of a Rig-Vedic hymn to one of the rain gods, Parjanya:

Come down hither with thy thunder, pouring out water, for thou, O Parjanya, art the living god, thou art our father.
Do thou roar, and thunder, and give fruitfulness. Fly around us with thy chariot full of water. Draw forth thy water-skin, when it has been opened and turned downwards, and let the high and low places become level.
Draw up the large bucket, and pour it out; let the streams pour forth freely. Soak heaven and earth with fatness, and let there be good draft for the cows.
Thou hast sent rain, stop now. Thou hast made deserts passable, thou hast made plants grow for food, and thou hast obtained praise from men.

Even in that distant past, probably about 3,000 years ago, when this hymn was composed, there was awareness that the monsoon brought both good and evil. But these two effects were reconciled by a moral notion. The same hymn said: 'When roaring and thundering thou killest evildoers, then everything rejoices, whatever lives on earth.' So the Vedic Aryan who saw how much good the monsoon did to him, did not like to make it a moral. He blamed death and destruction – at the hands of the monsoon – on himself, in so far as he was an evildoer. It was a clever way of thinking of the monsoon only with gratitude. Vedic sacrifices for rain are still performed. During some recent famines, enormous quantities of grain and ghee (melted butter), were thrown into a fire instead of being sent to relieve hunger.

Religion in India became associated with the monsoon in other ways as well. The festivals of the later cults of Hinduism are placed in the cycle of seasons, and the monsoon season has some of the most lyrical. These are, for example, those connected with the cult of the god Krishna whom Kipling described as the darling of the Gopi, 'the idol of dreaming maids and of mothers ere their children are born – Krishna the Well-beloved'. At the onset of the monsoon Krishna's car, known as the Juggernaut, is drawn and for the Hindus it has no fears. Later comes the festival of his birth in a dark night of rains, and of his swinging, when women and young girls in India go out and swing from the trees, singing all the time.

The impact of the monsoon is seen in literature and more especially in the poetry and fiction of love. Human life as a whole is ecological, and love between man and woman is still more so. Of this connection one of the earliest illustrations is the famous Sanskrit erotic poem, *Gita Govinda*, which opens with the line: 'The sky is soft with clouds.' Above all, the correlation is found in old and modern Bengali literature. There is a magical evocation in one old poem which tells of a girl sleeping with her sari all disheveled, but in unconscious happiness because of the soft rumble of the rain. Even in the Bengalis' most erotic poem a princess says to her husband-lover: 'During the rains we shall go a-boating up and down the river, and at night, clasped in each other's arms we shall listen to the rain and the wind.'

The most astonishing insight, largely subconscious, was shown by those modern Bengali writers who brought the idea of romantic love into our life. The most subtle feature of this assimilation was that each kind of love was placed in its appropriate setting of water. To give only one example, hopeless love in one of Tagore's stories is given its climax in a cyclone and storm surge.

A young man who had, in his patriotic resolve to dedicate his life to his country, rejected love – which might have been his for the asking – realized too late what he had given up. His love had become the wife of an elderly man and was living in the small country town near the sea coast where he was working as a school-teacher. He often went to see the husband, and could feel her presence behind the partitions. Of course, in our society there could be no question of meeting her.

One night, however, he heard the roar of the cyclone and the storm surge, and took shelter on a high bank. As he went up he saw another figure coming from the opposite side. It was his lost love. They stood side by side without exchanging one word, only staring at the waters swirling under the dark sky. The storm ceased, and the waters receded. Both of them went back to their houses. But for the young man those moments when they existed only for themselves were an eternity of bliss and love.

Monsoon and the life cycle

The festival of the goddess
Parvati is held during
India's great festival season
in August and September
when crops are ripening.

The rains bring love —
literally and ritually in
Jhulan, the happy, romantic
Festival of the Swings
dedicated to the god Krishna.

Women leave menfolk and
chores and 10,000 gather in the
Slave Garden of the Maharajah's
Palace in Udaipur to worship
the goddess Parvati.

Gond
Central India

Isolated by hill and forest
from the mainstream of
Hindu culture, women of
the Hill Marias leave their
breasts bare.

Among India's 585 million people, only some 30 million have held onto the ancient tribal cultures that prevailed before Hinduism took root. Of these tribal people the most numerous and, historically, most important is the large group of tribes known as the Gond.

Once the Gond were powerful rulers. As early as the dawn of the 15th century AD several Gond dynasties were firmly established in the regions now included within Madhya Pradesh and Maharashtra. The Gond rajas of that time were equal to many Hindu princes in power and material status, and the remnants of their forts speak of their former political importance. At the 73

Gond Central India

Gond girls are married at an early age and often leave their husbands later. Second or even third marriages are accepted in Gond society.

same time there were other Gond tribes who led the life of simple shifting cultivators in areas far removed from the centers of higher civilizations.

The tribal language of the Gond is an unwritten Dravidian tongue called Gondi, but less than half of the four million strong Gond speak it today. Those that do call themselves 'Koitur'. It is the Gond who have lost their own language and adopted such Aryan tongues as Hindi who describe themselves as 'Gond'. The Gond live scattered from the Vindhya mountains in the north to where the Godaveri river breaks through the eastern Ghats; in the states of Madhya Pradesh, Maharashtra, Andhra Pradesh and Orissa and neighboring states. They frequently live side by side with Hindu populations of varying linguistic and cultural backgrounds. They are not a homogenous people. Their economic development as well as their cultural traditions vary a great deal.

Except for the ruling families who were traditionally linked with specific localities – marked perhaps by some stone secular or religious structures – Gond have always been extremely mobile. Most of them have dwelt in hilly, sparsely populated country of cultivated areas separated by stretches of forest. Gond do not envisage their homes lasting for many years. They move from one site to

The Gond are traditionally farmers but add to their diet by fishing. Here women catch fish by hand from pools in a river they have dammed.

another for a variety of often trivial reasons. And so their timber and bamboo houses tend to be haphazardly arranged, possibly close together in streets and compact clusters, or scattered among kitchen gardens and fields.

House styles vary from region to region, but most Gond houses are rectangular buildings about twice as long as they are broad with a low thatched roof of grass and windowless mud walls. A 36-foot house is considered large, but whatever its size a Gond house has a veranda protected from rain and glare by low eaves. This is the men's favorite place to rest and work in during the hot weather, and it is where the family receives guests. Inside, most Gond houses are divided into a kitchen and a room where the family sleeps and the women work at grinding and pounding grain. There is little furniture in these rooms: in the main room one or two light cots, several low wooden tables, storage baskets and farm implements. Mats are used to sit and sleep on, but no Gond minds sitting on the floor. In the kitchen there are earthen and brass pots. A Gond family keeps its valuable possessions and stores of grain in the attic, reached from the kitchen by a bamboo ladder.

Most Gond tribespeople dress in the clothing worn by the lower cultivating castes of whatever region they live in. The men usually wear a loin-cloth of white cotton cloth, girded above the knees with a white or colored turban. Shirts have become popular recently, and so have coats tailored in western style. The Gond women wear nothing but a cotton sari, wrapped in such a way as to leave their legs, shoulders and the greater part of their bodies bare. They seldom wear bodices. Both men and women wear silver ornaments bought from professional silversmiths who produce heavy anklets and armlets specifically for the Gond.

The Gond are traditionally farmers and cattle breeders. They cultivate dry land where they grow various millets, maize and pulses as monsoon crops, and wheat, millet, cotton and oilseeds as winter crops. Gond myths and legends tell of chiefs plowing and herding cattle, and even today wealthy Gond do not disdain the work of the plowman. The Gond consider pottery and weaving to be beneath their dignity, but some work as carpenters and blacksmiths. A Gond does not think of agricultural work as a purely mechanical process as it is tied up with innumerable ritual observances. It is related to the worship of gods and spirits without whose blessing crops have no chance of prospering. Some of the simpler groups, such as the Hill Maria, still practise slash-and-burn cultivation but there are many indications that until fairly recently most Gond cultivated with hoes and digging-sticks on frequently shifted fields, and that the ox-drawn plow is a relatively recent innovation.

Their social system is diametrically opposed to their Hindu neighbors' hierarchy of caste groups and hereditary status distinctions. Most Gond groups are basically egalitarian. Even where there are still families of

chieftains who used to exert secular power, there has never been a rigid horizontal division between different social classes. Gond society presupposes the equality of all Gond in relation to intermarriage and participation in rites and ceremonies. This idea of equality is supported by a mythology which allows the Gond to view his society as an integrated and self-sufficient whole. Whereas every Hindu caste sees itself as part of a complex society, consisting of many mutually dependent but inherently different components, Gond society is a universe on its own, independent of other communities.

Though Gond society appears as indivisible to the outside world, it is in fact elaborately structured. It consists of a limited number of clans which have a clearly defined social and ritual relationship to each other. The position of every individual within this system is fixed and determines many aspects of his relationships with other Gond. This unalterable position of the individual in the scheme of clans extends beyond the limits of this earthly life into the Land of the Dead, where the members of a clan are supposed to join their ancestors and to live forever in the company of their clan-deity. A man's place in the system cannot be changed either by his own actions or by those of a village council or other tribunal, for even if he is temporarily deprived of his tribal privileges he remains a member of his clan.

Although the Gond clan system is rigid there are no rules governing who lives where. A village community consists of the village-founder or his descendants, his kinsmen who joined in the foundation of the village, and all those who at any later point in time decided to settle in the village. Such a community is extremely unstable, for families may move away and settle in neighboring villages for no strong reason. Marriage also tends to be unstable. Many girls who are married at an early age, often without any preceding courtship, leave their husbands and seek other partners. The Gond tend to take a tolerant view of sexual irregularities, and a wife's adultery arouses little indignation. If she has left her marital home and has gone to live with a lover, the husband will usually try to persuade her to return to him. Only if she refuses to come back and wishes to marry her lover, will he insist on divorce and compensation. Divorced and widowed women remarry frequently and women living with a second or third husband lose no respect. Men may have several wives at a time, and have therefore less incentive to part from the woman to whom they were married in their early youth.

Among the Gond of Bastar marriages are more stable. These Gond have youth dormitories and in these boys and girls enjoy for some years a life of sexual permissiveness. They also learn the need for civic responsibility, for the organization of these dormitories, which also have the role of youth clubs, lies in the hands of the young people themselves, and no adult is permitted to interfere.

People of Calcutta
Bengal

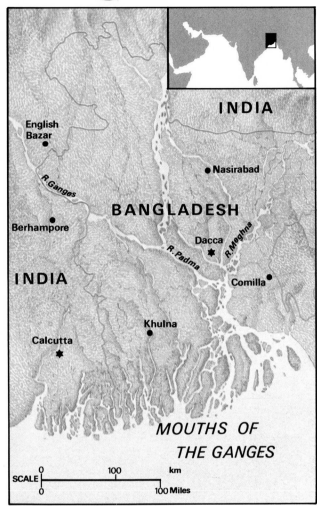

INDIA

English
Bazar

R. Ganges

Nasirabad

BANGLADESH

Berhampore

Dacca

R. Padma

R. Meghna

INDIA

Comilla

Khulna

Calcutta

MOUTHS OF
THE GANGES

SCALE

0   100   km

0   100 Miles

Calcutta is India's most arrogant city. By all accounts, and particularly those of the Bengalis, what Calcutta thinks today India thinks tomorrow. This claim, even if not totally devoid of truth, is scarcely guaranteed to endear Bengalis to the rest of their allegedly less-gifted countrymen. The erstwhile Bengali *Babu* (sir), delighting to engage in philosophical discourse upon the most esoteric subjects, views his neighbors from other Indian states with undisguised disdain. He finds the Bihari a trifle uncouth; the Punjabi positively bohemian; and the Madrasi agreeable enough but basically dull. Confronted with the decaying city of Calcutta, his neighbors may with justifiable derision wonder just where Bengali genius has invested itself. The Bengali response is both amusing and sad. He affects the air of an aristocrat who has fallen upon hard times, but is confident his style will out in the end. Rather in the manner of the English, a people incidentally with whom the Bengalis share many faults, he is given to the copious analysis of his own shortcomings but fiercely resents anyone else's attempt to do the same.

The Maidan, a park built as
a buffer between Calcutta
and British troops in Fort
William, is now the scene of
frequent political meetings.

(Left) Bengalis have a high regard for scholarship and learning. Government clerks work in the euphemistically named Writers' Building.

Tolly's Nullah, the oldest drainage canal in Calcutta, is being rebuilt. But half the city is unsewered and open drains are often choked.

(Bottom) Calcutta University, with 200,000 students, is the world's largest degree factory —and an explosive center of learning.

Calcutta is the wealthiest city in India in terms of sheer accumulated capital – a distinct hangover from its days as 'the second city of the British empire'. It is home as well as headquarters to the Birla family whose all-pervasive, all-powerful position in the Indian scheme of things is very possibly unmatched anywhere else in the world. They own or have controlling interests in Hindustan Motors; *Hindustan Times,* a national newspaper; Indian Shipping Co Ltd; the Hindustan Investment Corporation Ltd; Jayashree Textiles Ltd; Minerals and Minerals Ltd; Textile Machinery Corporation Ltd; Universal Electric Co Ltd; Universal Cables Ltd; and the Usha Development Co Ltd, to mention but a few of their companies. For their relaxation they maintain an ice-rink at home which operates even when the outside temperature is around 100 degrees fahrenheit, which it frequently is in Calcutta during the summer months. While the Birlas live not uncomfortably, life for the other seven million residents of Calcutta has set new limits in human endurance. The juxtaposition of unimaginable wealth with a kind of degradation that is almost unbelievable even when seen, so shattering is its effect on the uninitiated, has produced an urban time-bomb.

Outside the *Grand* or the *Great Eastern* hotels, the pavement is littered with the prostrate bodies of cripples, beggars, at night sleeping humanity, and always with hawkers selling everything from Chinese fountain pens and garish pictures of Indian gods and film stars to airmail editions of foreign newspapers. At Sham Bazar in north Calcutta, meeting point of five roads and many more philosophies, and next-door in College Street, self-styled poets, writers, painters and talkers sidestep the jangling trams and roaring buses to gather at the tea shops, more often than not called coffee houses, to exchange endless gossip over interminable cups of tea. As dusk settles over Calcutta, the flower-sellers carelessly toss their garlands of flowers over the crash barriers at street corners. Office workers returning home stop to buy the perfumed flowers for their wives to wear in their hair, thus enhancing female beauty and masculine desire. In the markets the smell of the new clothes hung from shop fronts mingles with a thousand other scents, the odor of openly-dumped refuse, the perfume of the flowers and joss-sticks, and all this overlaid by an overwhelming sense of chaos creates that elusive something which the natives of Calcutta call life.

Two hundred years of continuous British presence has left a curious legacy in Calcutta. The tangible ones, such as the Victoria Memorial Hall, built of white marble in the image of the Taj Mahal, are easier to explain. Termed 'Curzon's Folly' at first, after the viceroy who built this monument, it has become a meeting place for coy lovers, as well as for peasants who flock in their thousands from the villages every year to stare at pictures of Queen Victoria, one-time Empress of India.

The Bengali temperament, with its excessively high

79

Many people in Calcutta have no home except the streets. A Christian charity picks up the dying at dawn in a truck, to give them final comfort.

(Bottom) In the darkness of a Calcutta jute mill the workers' sweat contributes to the humidity necessary for the production of the fiber.

(Right) In the heart of Calcutta industrious workers turn rooftops into factory floors and fill quilts and mattresses with raw cotton.

regard for learning and scholarship, was particularly receptive to the international outlook on life that the British brought with them. The fusion of liberal ideas from Europe onto a Bengali superstructure led directly to the growth of nationalism, and this eventually proved to be the undoing of British rule in India. Whether the critical decision in 1835 to introduce the widespread teaching of English would have been taken had the British foreseen the rise of Bengali nationalism is highly doubtful. Essentially it was the lure of trade which first drew the British, in the form of the East India Company, to Calcutta. As Britain's economic interests swelled political power inevitably had to follow to secure the trading concessions which had been won by all possible means from fierce battle to doubtful diplomacy.

Calcutta's beginning, in so far as it has a clear one, came to pass in 1690 when Job Charnock, an agent of the East India Company, set up shop by the villages of Sutanati, Govindpur, and Kalikata near the River Hoogly, a branch of the Ganges. The climate may have been too humid, and possibly a little unhealthy, but of the advantages of Calcutta's location as a port near the Bay of Bengal there was little doubt. Calcutta's hinterland extends today to an estimated 237,000 square miles comprising, apart from West Bengal, the states of Assam, Bihar, Manipur, Tripura, Nagaland, and part of Orissa and Uttar Pradesh. Until the recent industrial unrest the port of Calcutta handled 40 per cent of India's foreign trade. Calcutta is also the major financial center of India. Roughly a quarter of the total bank loans in India are made by the Calcutta banks. The British made Calcutta the hub of their commercial activity in India, and this is what it has remained.

The consolidation of British power in India came in 1757 after the historic battle of Plessey. Robert Clive, an impetuous Englishman whose grasp of administrative and military matters had escaped notice at home, defeated the Nawab of Bengal, Siraj-ud-Dowlah. The Nawab had been a marked man ever since the notorious Black Hole incident of the previous year. Into the Nawab's hands had fallen the hapless British residents of Fort William in Calcutta. Somewhere between 146 and 164 people (the precise number has been the subject of much debate) were confined on a hot June night to a badly-ventilated room, 18 feet by 15 feet. The following morning only 23 emerged alive. The incident was destined to cling to the very name of Calcutta for ever afterwards. This kind of cruelty did not characterize the British period in India, but it was by no means the most callous affair to be perpetrated during this period. That was a record left for General Dyer to achieve in 1919 when troops under his command shot and killed 379 Indians, including women and children, at a protest meeting at Jallianawalla Bagh in Amritsar. After this massacre, most Indian opinion swung round to the feeling that had long been current in Calcutta. This was the unequivocal demand for total

(Over page) The population of Calcutta and its environs is expected to reach 60 million by 1990. It began as a trading port in the 18th century.

independence from Britain. In between the two landmarks of Plassey and Jallianawalla Bagh, the British empire waxed and waned.

The spread of knowledge through the English language has affected Bengali life in a profound way. With the founding of colleges in Calcutta the city became a center of learning. Colleges were founded in quick succession, and great strides taken in education. Hindu College was founded in 1817. The name had unhealthy connotations and was changed in 1855 to Presidency College. Presidency rapidly became the most distinguished and powerful Calcutta college, soon earning a reputation as the 'Balliol of the East'. Other colleges followed. Calcutta University was established in 1857 and today has jurisdiction over 200 colleges and 200,000 students, making it the largest degree-producing machine in the world. Very possibly it is also the world's most explosive university.

English made a tremendous impact on Bengali education. Not everyone of course approved of the changes. Priyaranjan Sen, a professor, complained 'One of the evils which attended English education in its initial stage was drink.' The summing up on the changes ushered in by English was fairer. Baruda Charan Mitra, a member of the Bengal Judicial Service, wrote in the *Calcutta Review* in 1885 'Thus we have western influence coming to Bengal mainly through the medium of English and spreading by means of education; popular newspapers; busy law courts; even through environment; these being some of the channels of communication.'

Whatever the individual reactions, the scene had been set in Calcutta for the appearance of some of the most prominent men of modern India. One of the first figures of the Bengali renaissance was Raja Rammohan Roy (1772-1833), described by the poet Rabindranath Tagore as the 'greatest man of modern India'. Rammohan Roy came from a once-wealthy family of *zamindars*, as the feudal landlords in Bengal are called. He was a man of extraordinary scholarship, and played a leading role in the founding of Hindu College. But he was strongly opposed to the narrower aspects of Hinduism, such as the conventional worship of gods and goddesses, the caste, and above all, *suttee*. This was the practice whereby a Hindu wife found life so intolerable on the death of her husband that she cast herself voluntarily into the flames of his funeral pyre. That was the ideal. In reality the wife was invariably dragged screaming and kicking to the burning grounds, showing a most unworthy desire to live. It is recorded that between 1815-1817, for example, 983 women were burnt alive with their husband's corpses in Calcutta. This colorful local custom was banned by Lord William Bentinck, Governor-General of Bengal, in 1829.

Rammohan Roy also started the Brahmo Samaj, a movement for social and religious reform. The sect included a number of Bengali intellectuals, among them the distinguished Tagore family, but it aroused substan-

At the Kali temple pilgrims and priests perform rites for their ancestors and toss incense, marigolds and butter over countless fires.

Mother Teresa's help for the sick and destitute grew world-famous. Her 'Home for the Dying' is behind the temple of Kali—goddess of destruction.

85

The sacred thread circles the chest of a holy man during prayer rites of Durga Puja, Calcutta's principal festival.

People of Calcutta Bengal

In Calcutta there is always
traffic congestion. Buses
built for 80 carry 130
passengers—and not all
of them inside.

In Calcutta the Communist
party is a powerful force.
Politics are often violent.
No big election has yet
occurred without a few deaths.

Many *marwari*—members of India's commercial class—are richer men than they seem. Much gold is privately hoarded in Calcutta and elsewhere too.

tial hostility from conservative Hindus. One of the sidelights was that the Brahmo Samaj had no objections to their followers eating beef, in direct contradiction of one of the strongest taboos of the Hindu religion. Nor were widows allowed to marry, in spite of the abolition of *suttee*. The cause was taken up by, among others, Pandit Iswar Chandra Vidyasagar (1820-1901), a renowned scholar, who also campaigned against child marriage and polygamy. On widow remarriage he dissipated public prejudice by quoting from the old Hindu scriptures that the marriage of widows was permitted by the *Shastras* (ancient Hindu law). His book *Should widows marry?* became something of a best-seller. Two thousand copies were sold outright, and a second edition of 3,000 copies was also snapped up like hot curry. Motilal Seal, a respected Bengali, was even moved to offer 'a gift of 10,000 rupees (worth about $1,250 now but at least ten times as much in the mid-19th century) to any Hindu who would dare to marry a widow of his own faith'. Under such pressure from the big boys of Bengal the Widow Marriage Act was passed in 1856, but to this day Hindu widows tend not to remarry.

The Bengali renaissance threw up a number of literary giants who contributed to the pattern of Bengali thinking. The tradition persists so that all year round in Calcutta, and especially during the festivals, the bookstalls flood over to the pavements with local produce. Most educated Bengalis wish to get into print, and will frequently pay to have their work published. The writing that characterized the renaissance was essentially lyrical, and its appeal gives the outsider an insight into the romantic strain in the Bengali nature. Bengali developed as a soft and beautiful language which could not only reflect the new stirrings of nationalism but also express the subtler nuances of human emotion.

The greatest figure of the Bengali renaissance was Rabindranath Tagore, Bengal's best loved son. He was born into a family where western ways had become taboo. He displayed a facility with words from a precocious age and had plenty of opportunity to develop his talents later when he looked after the family estates outside Calcutta. His duties were not excessively arduous; in any case he was usually lost in the admiration of rural Bengal, and wrote songs and poems to suit the different seasons. Among the flowers and trees of Santiniketan, a village not far from Calcutta, he founded a school for the teaching of the arts. Lessons were always held in the open unless interrupted by a monsoon shower. He broke away from the rigid ideas held on education, and tried to develop a more relaxed master-pupil relationship. Santiniketan was, in effect, the precursor of the modern art workshop. Tagore gave Santiniketan – the school was soon upgraded to the University of Vishwavarati – his individual stamp, and soon its fame had spread all over India. Indira Gandhi, the Indian Prime Minister was educated here. It was at Santiniketan that Tagore wrote

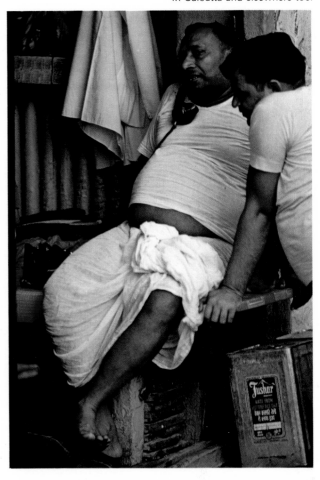

Gitanjali, acknowledged as his masterpiece. He had written a great deal besides, essays, novels, plays – but it is his poetry that is sublime. *Gitanjali* (an offering of songs) compounded the peculiarly Bengali outlook on life into verse. For Tagore there followed adulation from all over India and international recognition.

In 1913 Rabindranath Tagore was awarded the Nobel Prize for Literature, the first Indian to be awarded the honor. After *Gitanjali* Calcutta knew that whatever else followed Bengalis could always hold their heads up high. Bengali culture had arrived; not only that, it had established itself as one of the world's great cultures. By the time Tagore died in 1941 he had published an estimated 150,000 lines in verse and plays, compared with Milton's 18,000, and his prose ran to about twice that amount. In his sixties he took up painting. He also established a whole new school of music called *Rabindra Sangeet* (the music of Rabindra). No evening in Calcutta now passes without the performance of *Rabindra Sangeet* somewhere or other.

It is not however for its art that the world recognizes Calcutta. No less an authority on the subject than Lenin 87

People of Calcutta Bengal

Many men in Calcutta have
left wives and families at
home in distant villages. Out
of such insecurity, the nostrum
vendors make a good living.

Jamini Roy, the grand old
man of Bengali painting,
died in 1972. Calcutta
has a flourishing artistic
and literary culture.

himself is reported to have remarked 'The road to revolution lies through Peking, Shanghai and Calcutta.' The authorship of the remark is sometimes disputed but it does not really matter: the sentiment is clear. The inability of the majority of Calcutta's residents to secure even the most basic fundamentals of life has led to extreme frustration. This is all the more intolerable because of their background and consequently greater expectations from life. The phenomenon of a highly educated but impoverished middle class is not unique to Calcutta, but is present here in an exceptionally acute form. Of 500,000 who registered themselves as being unemployed at the employment exchange in Calcutta recently, no less than 200,000 were educated with school-leaving certificates, or higher qualifications. This is in a nation where three out of four people are illiterate. The graduates who do find employment more often than not accept positions far below what would suit their capabilities and education. Bus drivers these days are invariably graduates. Vacancies when advertized, even for menial jobs, attract an overwhelming response. The lure of higher education remains, partly for its own sake, and partly because there is not much else to do.

In spite of Calcutta's dominant position as the center of commerce and industry, a succession of central Indian governments in New Delhi have ignored Calcutta. Calcutta Municipal Corporation became so utterly inept at discharging its function that it ultimately had to be suspended, and its duties taken over by the West Bengal government. Nearly half of Calcutta is unsewered. The increase in population has meant that the open drains get more easily choked. During the monsoons even a moderate downpour is guaranteed to flood some streets, and with many tramlines submerged traffic is badly dislocated. The traffic problems have got steadily worse. Buses meant for 80 carry 130 passengers on average, and trams for 50 carry 85. The total number of public transport vehicles has actually declined over the years. From 666 buses and 410 trams in 1963, the numbers decreased to 593 buses and 350 trams in 1969. Nothing took their place. Latterly some effort has been made to deal with the traffic situation. Work has begun on an underground railway system with Russian help, the target for completion being 1978. There is a plan to build a second bridge over the River Hoogly, but there have been such suggestions before. Other environmental problems include the disposal of rubbish from the street. Over two thousand tons of it are dumped daily onto the streets, and only three-quarters of it can be removed when the corporation works at full stretch (which normally it doesn't).

One can see why the restlessness which infests Calcutta is aggravated by living conditions. But there is a political background, too, to explain Calcutta's perpetually volatile mood. Lord Curzon, the viceroy, divided Bengal in 1905 into East Bengal, with a mainly Muslim popu-

lation, and West Bengal, with a mainly Hindu population. The Muslims had been the traditional ruling class in Bengal until the arrival of the British. They lost their advantage by generally avoiding the schools and universities which the British founded in Calcutta, while the Hindus seized the opportunities with great enthusiasm. Partition caused such a furore that in 1911 it had to be revoked. The following year the British got their own back. The capital was shifted from Calcutta to Delhi, thus degrading Calcutta's political importance. The damage from the British point of view had been done; the nationalist movement had spread to other parts of India. Calcutta leaders tended by and large to be on the left of the Congress Party's campaign for independence.

No one epitomized the spirit of the Bengalis better than Subhas Chandra Bose (1897-1945), a born rebel if ever there was one. He found the political strategies of both Nehru and Gandhi much too slow for his liking. Negotiating held little attraction for him; in simple terms, he wanted the British booted out. Subhas Bose was educated at Presidency College, Calcutta and at Fitzwilliam House, Cambridge. Unlike Nehru, he appeared to have no obvious weakness for the English. From Cambridge he wrote home to declare that 'what gives me the greatest joy is to see the whiteskins serving me and cleaning my shoes.' His plan, in which he included Japanese support for his Indian National Army, never materialized after the Japanese advance into Southeast Asia was checked by British forces. Bose died, very probably in 1945, in circumstances which have never been quite established. There are people in Calcutta, and some of them are not cranks, who firmly refuse to believe that Netaji (the great leader, as he was known) is dead. They say he is biding his time in some friendly country, and will return one day to redeem his people.

Politics in Calcutta has become much more involved, and considerably more passionate, since the days of Subhas Bose and his contemporaries. India's independence in 1947 was accompanied by the partition of Bengal for a second time. West Bengal with its industrial complexes remained in India. East Bengal with its rich fishing grounds, jute fields, and fertile lands became East Pakistan. Communal strife in 1946 and 1947 saw unrestrained butchery by both sides in Punjab, which had been also severed, and in Bengal. When the carnage was over, one million men, women and children had been killed. In 25 years since independence the scars of Hindu-Muslim communalism have largely healed. Albeit a steady stream of Hindu refugees from East Pakistan into India, and of Muslim refugees in the reverse direction, has been maintained. The civil war between West Pakistan and East Bengal in 1971 saw an additional ten million refugees flood into West Bengal, stretching Calcutta's limited resources nearly to breaking point. The successful secession of East Pakistan from the Islamic Republic of Pakistan, and the emergence of 89

Almost everyone in Calcutta celebrates Durga Puja, the festival to the goddess of the city. Here women smear vermilion on their faces.

(Top) Calcutta is India's richest city and home as well as headquarters to many of India's wealthiest families of financiers and industrialists.

The Royal Calcutta Turf Club is a legacy of the time when the city was 'the second city of the British empire'. Here the rich view Derby Day races.

Bangladesh as a sovereign independent state was an unexpected and welcome development for Calcutta. It has raised the prospects of co-operation between Calcutta and Dacca, so that some of the damage caused by partition may be repaired.

The Bangladesh cause had been taken up enthusiastically by the people of Calcutta. It pushed to a side Calcutta's own politics, including the activities of the Naxalites, originally a breakaway Marxist group, which had as its objective a bloody peasant revolution. Essentially a romantic uprising which gained ground in the 1960s, it culminated in an open Naxalite-Marxist war which produced several thousand political murders. The movement attracted students, but not the middle class. It failed because the violence which gripped West Bengal finally appalled and sickened even the people for whom the movement was intended. Calm has since come to Calcutta, but continuing frustration is reflected in the daily demonstrations and in the single cry: *Biplab* (revolution).

Calcutta is the city of Satyajit Ray, India's internationally celebrated film director. Ray's passion, so evident in his famous trilogy *Pather Panchali, Aparajito* and *Apur Sansar*, for depicting the truth, plus his gift for capturing

A handful of rich merchant families—one of which owns the Marble Palace, built in Greco-Roman splendor — have survived India's egalitarianism.

People of Calcutta Bengal

Calcutta is the home of sitar
music and the principal
musicians are Bengalis. Here
a sitar is polished in one
of the many factories.

Satyajit Ray, Calcutta's world famous film maker, improvises with pre-war equipment. The city is home to many artists and writers.

During Kali Puja, a festival to the goddess of destruction, clay images of demons are sold to be placed alongside images of Kali herself.

the quintessence of the Bengali character, has brought promise of a second Bengali renaissance. But one should confess that Hindi films, produced in Bombay, have a much wider appeal in Calcutta. Their dance sequences, rhythmic music and unlikely romances, and overt sexual innuendos (even though kissing on the Indian screen is still not shown) packs the halls in Calcutta.

Calcutta proliferates with small, mostly amateur drama groups. Nearly all offices have their own groups. Productions tend to favor the melodramatic. Cynics see this as an attempt to compensate for a lack of excitement in the actual lives of the actors. Calcutta has of late seen a tremendous revival of *Jatra*, the traditional traveling theater, which requires only an open space to stage a performance. Experimental theater has its adherents, but mainly of the sophisticated. A good example of this is the Little Theater group. Its actor-director, Utpal Dutt, has ruffled many establishment feathers with such productions as *Angar* (Burning Coal), a play based on exploitation in a coal mine, and *Kallol* (Wave), which is about a mutiny on a ship. Their veiled suggestions to the audience were clear, or so it seemed to a West Bengal government. Soon after *Kallol's* open air performance in a Calcutta field, Utpal Dutt was flung into jail for a few months.

In spite of pressure from so many directions, the people of Calcutta have retained a sense of humor. This has probably been their salvation. To be able to enjoy life even in the midst of such chaos is a quality that cannot be taken for granted. The greatest social and religious event of the Bengali calendar is *Durga Puja*, a festival in October given over to the worship of the Mother Goddess. The shops do brisk business; it is estimated that nearly half of all clothing bought during the year is sold during these few days. Each *para*, or locality, in Calcutta has its own statue, built to specification, of Durga, the benign smiling Mother Goddess. With a great flurry of fire-crackers and a beating of drums, Durga is borne to her pedestal to be watched, admired and worshipped for three days by passing humanity. There is much competition between different *paras* to have the brightest and best statue. Those three days are filled with ceaseless activity – social, cultural and religious. Bengalis who never have a single holy thought during the rest of the year do so now. At the end of the three days Durga is borne away to the Mother Ganges, mother of the world, tossed into the waters and delivered unto her. Thus the Bengali voyage begins again through the travails of the coming year to yet another *Durga Puja*.

The Bengali dream is compounded of noble thoughts and little action, of scholarship but scant physical application. And the humor is always there. When India beat England at cricket at the Oval in 1972 Calcutta went delirious. The people spontaneously declared it a holiday. It was the kind of impetuous but intensely human behavior which goes to make Calcutta Calcutta.

Sikhs
Harijana, Punjab and Delhi

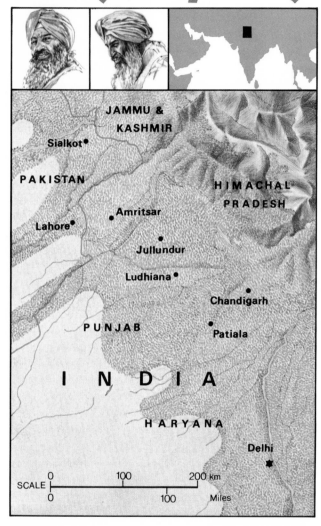

The Punjab is a land of flat, square fields crisscrossed by a network of turquoise blue canals and treelined roads. The world knows one of its communities, the Sikhs, particularly well: tall men whose walk resembles the swaying of wheat just before the harvest; reckless and bold men whose nature knows no worry. In summer dust and heat, on damp dewy winter mornings, these romantic figures roamed up to Attock and Peshawar fighting and conquering. For the Punjab was undivided then. Its wide flat plains made travel easy and gave men a feeling of space.

As a region the Punjab remained separate from the rest of the sub-continent. It had a different social structure from Hindu India: social and political relations were defined not by castes and by ideas of purity and pollution, but by families, their honor, and the coalitions they established with each other to defend that honor.

In 1947 west Punjab became the Muslim homeland of Pakistan. In November 1966 the Indian Punjab was divided so as to secure a Sikh majority area in the central Punjab. Since 1947 the Punjab has been only a memory.

There are rather more than ten million Sikhs. Until the 19th century the Sikh community was predominantly rural. The Jats, the ancestral landowners in the rural areas of the Punjab, have a family tradition of administrative and army service and political control of the province's affairs. It is common to find generations of soldiering in one family and of administrative service in another. Non-Jats, the Sikhs who live in towns, and who are recent converts to Sikhism, control India's motor spare parts industry and are prominent in trade and business in all of India's cities. All Sikh men, Jat or non-Jat, have the common last name of Singh – lion, and all Sikh women the common last name Kaur – princess. When Sikhs meet, they say to each other *Sat Sri Akal* – God is Truth. A Sikh enters into a union of equality with all the other members of his community when he goes through a ceremony known as *pahul,* gate. In the presence of five initiated members of the community his face is sprinkled with sweet water, *amrit,* which is also drunk to shouts of 'We are God's chosen; victory be to our God'. Holy food called *pershad,* a mixture of equal amounts of flour, sugar and clarified butter, is distributed to all present and eaten together. Jats tended to take *amrit* only when entering military service or before a battle: it represented a commitment by whole regiments to fight to the death, united by what they believed to be sacred – their community and their valor.

The Sikhs' religion is as bare and clear as their plains and their unclouded sky. They believe in one god, revealed to them in the teachings of the ten *gurus* – prophets whose writings are contained in the holy book, the *Granth Sahib,* written in the Gurumukhi script. In the Sikhs' houses too, man is unhindered in his direct approach to god by a proliferation of objects. Behind the high walls of large square houses with closed iron gates, there is little except *razaiyees* – heavy down quilts, *charpoys* – string beds, and steel trunks storing family valuables.

Non-Jats define themselves as Sikhs by their strict religious observance, by rigorously and attentively wearing the five Sikh symbols: *kirpan* – a steel dagger, *kara* – a steel bangle, *kanghha* – a comb, *kes* – uncut hair and *kachchh* – short breeches, and by daily temple-going and by their habit of keeping a room in their house for the *Granth Sahib.* They initiate their children between the ages of 12 and 18. Jats are less devout. In hot weather, no matter who is present, a Jat will take off his turban as if it were a hat, unashamedly wandering around home, village and fields with his hair exposed. Jat villages do not always have a *gurudwara* (temple) and even if they did, there would be no weekly services, nor would any Jat feel obliged to attend. A Jat's sense of identity is so strong that he would still regard himself as a Sikh even if he no longer wore the symbols nor believed in Sikhism. His sense of being a Sikh is defined in the gift of his life,

Map labels: JAMMU & KASHMIR, Sialkot, PAKISTAN, HIMACHAL PRADESH, Amritsar, Lahore, Jullundur, Ludhiana, Chandigarh, PUNJAB, Patiala, INDIA, HARYANA, Delhi, SCALE, 0 100 200 km, 0 100 Miles

95

Through New Delhi streets
rides a living symbol of the
khalsa, the martial fraternity
of Sikhs, marked by his uncut
hair, steel bangle and dagger.

the possession of his sacred land and his inherited attachment to fighting to defend and rule that land.

Each morning, while a city Sikh takes an hour or so pressing his beard, tying his turban and pacing up and down the courtyard reading his *gutka* (a pocket *Granth Sahib*), Jats are involved in very different activities: planning a political conspiracy, making a marriage, supervising laborers, attending court on a land dispute. Rather than go to the *gurudwara* themselves, Jats will take the *Granth Sahib* over to a land-owner's house for a prayer-reading attended by all the villagers who are treated as guests and served with food after the prayers.

It is only in very specific circumstances that the Sikh community mobilizes itself in terms of its religious bonds. Sikhs define themselves as a religious community, and emphasize their separate religious heritage because their community is incorporated within what they regard as a Hindu India, while on their western border are Muslim lands. Since the 15th century Sikhs have fought and defended themselves against Muslims. Sikh history is a statement of their devotion to their cultural values, a symbol of their difference from the two neighboring communities.

A Sikh child does not learn of his heroic tradition, of brave ancestors who fought and died for the community, at school or from elderly family members. The events of the past are proudly recited twice daily, at sunrise and sunset, in the *Ardas,* a community prayer service which in the evening usually closes with the words 'The Khalsa shall reign supreme and none shall be kept in subjection. Those who seek protection shall be saved.' Sikhs believe these verses embody the goal towards which their community still strives, a sovereign Sikh state. The words are an emotional link with their past when they were rulers of the Punjab.

For centuries Sikh lives were devoted to regaining lost possessions and taking new ones. The successful efforts of Sikh farmers who were dispossessed from what is now Pakistan to turn the east Punjab from an area with a food shortage into an area with a food surplus feeding a large part of India, is a part of Sikh tradition. Their ruthless determination to regain any personal loss – of possessions, family or friends – is the result of Sikh historical experience. The attitude is expressed by one man who said 'You decide a thing and then go ahead with it, thunder or storm. A thousand tempests should not stop you!' Sikhs prefer occupations which involve constant physical activity – whether as an administrator touring a district, as a policeman dashing after border smugglers or as an army officer on active service. In the music in the *gurudwaras* or temple hymns, the *kirtan*, echo the rhythms of mind and being. They are swift, decided and not meditational. The Sikh temperament has been the most important factor in their province's development into India's richest state.

Their semi-nomadic tradition has also continued from past to present. Jats are doctors, engineers, agricultural specialists and migrant laborers in foreign countries. Others are traders in the Middle East, Turkey and Iran. Emigration has replaced the Jat tradition of service in foreign armies. For all Sikhs it is in accordance with their tradition of roaming in search of opportunity.

Jats and non-Jats remain separated by divergent economic interests, which also have political significance and, more important, by Jat family traditions. City Sikhs in the past intermarried with Hindu fellow-traders and businessmen and do not as a result share the Jat practice of *karewa* by which a woman marries her brother-in-law after her husband's death. Men and women in a city family eat together, and value a close relationship between man and wife. There is no customary law, as among the Jats, that binds them to divide their property equally among their sons. City Sikhs give their spare wealth to the *gurudwaras,* whereas Jats use wealth to gain political support and to increase family honor. Jats can have neither political position nor honor unless they dispense with their wealth.

Jats and non-Jats have different attitudes to death. City Sikhs accept death only when it occurs in war, or as a result of illness or old age. But among Jats, especially in border areas where feuding persists, death is a fact of the moment. After the 1965-1966 war with Pakistan a Jat landlord and army officer said 'The threat and danger of death to those dear to us has now gone. Yet our mentality is such that we will always expect invasion. While peace lasts in our family and in our village, we build up our wealth. When war comes or political rivalries are resumed our wealth and our sons are lost.' One winter 28 bullet wounds were found in the body of one of my husband's close relatives. I was horrified, and so were my Sikh friends in the city who thought it brutal. But my Jat relatives merely said '*Bhabiji* (sister-in-law), you should not be worried. Murders keep on happening. It is the Jat way of life.' The temple ceremony that followed was more a demonstration of political allegiances than of personal mourning.

There is a saying among Jats that they are all one family. Any family can connect itself to most other Jat families. Jats do not hesitate to marry out when it is to their distinct financial advantage to do so, but since political and landed power circulates mainly within their section of the community, they tend to strengthen their ties with each other. And one of the most important ways of showing friendship is for a man to make marriage alliances for his friends.

From childhood men are taught to expect emotional sustenance from mother, brothers and friends. They can embrace their mothers publicly, and walk along the street hand in hand with their friends. From his wife a Jat does not expect love, but sons to continue his family line. He also expects help, not only from her immediate family but from the whole network of people to whom

Sikhs crowd outside the *gurdwara* awaiting the arrival of the relics of Guru Gobind Singh, taken to England in 1849 after the Anglo-Sikh wars.

(Bottom) Gobind Singh initiated the *khalsa* – the pure – as an army of soldier-saints dedicated to fighting for their reformed Hinduism.

she is attached through her brothers, sisters and cousins.

The ties of friendship between men make romantic love unacceptable. In the Punjab a young woman loved is regarded as a destructive force and no dignity is attached to this love. One aristocratic Jat explained 'Passion and desire which beautiful women arouse lead to the corruption of the soul in sex and to the destruction of friendship between brothers.' 'Brothers' here includes cousins and close male friends. Men spend little time with their wives. They are out all day and usually spend the evenings with their friends. Women are not lonely, for their companions are their children. A mother's most intense relationship is with her son, who generally sleeps with her until he is twelve. Sons are not only her sole source of affection. They are her supporters, fighting against her husband, their father, and the similar attachment he has with his own mother. Indeed one Jat's definition of a good Jat is 'he who bashes up his father, is independent, with his own property, and keeps some weapons and a few men around him.' Sons are frequently so devoted to their mother that they will plan to beat up or even kill their father for troubling her. Sons have even been known to express their hatred against their father by planning to kill his mother, especially if the old woman is rich. But in families with many children some would sleep with their grandmother and develop bonds with her rather than with their own mother.

Families control resources. A family's political position, in village, state or locality is maintained, and its wealth protected, by its associations with other families who are friendly for their own purposes and interests. All that is important to a man – the protection of his family honor in the eyes of other families – could be managed only through his membership of a *paarti* or faction which would protect his interests politically at state level. Jats in the Punjab rural areas believe 'everyone is my neighbor who is my friend'. The Jats are friends with those who will help them. In any landlord's house on any one evening will be a gathering of such diverse people as smugglers, politicians, high-ranking police officers, lawyers, land revenue officers and businessmen, bound only by what each can offer the other. Sikhs believe all men are approachable, and social relationships are desirable with all men. By commanding a sphere of influence a man has the independence and freedom by which he is equal to any man. Without this freedom he would be subject to insult. And if a man is insulted he is lowered, no longer equal with his fellows.

A man frequently makes enemies in his efforts to promote not only his friends' but also his own family's well-being. By excelling the achievements of neighboring families he insults them. They must defend their honor by arranging jointly with other interested families to oppose him, in conformity with the principle of reciprocity in all matters, or *izzat*. A man frequently finds his friends in terms of his enemies. Because of the widespread network of friendships and alliances, which are as open and unlimited as the Punjab plains, enmities are rarely confined to one area. Soon a man will find he is opposed by a state-wide network, including, as well as his original opponents, their friends in their capacities as policemen, magistrates and politicians. His resources, his position, even his life, may be at risk.

Jats are more heavily committed to their personal network of friends and family than they are concerned about ideas. They are concerned only with who possesses them. Members of opposing political parties may nevertheless have no political differences because they are friends and therefore bound to support each other regardless of party allegiances. In other societies men have been deformed, and have betrayed their friends, by their devotion to abstract ideas. With the Jat Sikh, the situation is reversed. A man who has insulted him or killed one of his friends can have no philosophy or merit. The Jats were unable to mobilize to support a particularly able Jat Chief Minister – Kairon – in his efforts to develop the Punjab – their Punjab. He was not a friend to all Jats and therefore could not universally be supported. He was assassinated as an act of private vengeance. 97

Kashmiri
Kashmir

Kashmir's beauty once inspired
a Mogul emperor to exclaim 'If
indeed there be heaven on the
face of the earth it is here,
it is here, here it is!'

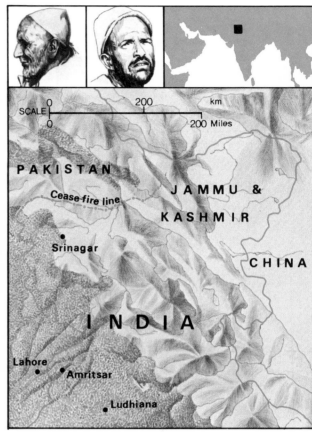

At Srinagar, in the Valley of Kashmir, the soft sun of a late afternoon makes the waters of Dal lake seem clear and the mountains steep and close. The town of Srinagar is cut by a network of jeweled waterways where *shikaras* like Venetian gondolas slip along with a gently rocking motion. Boulevards along the shore are quiet as the evening draws on. Only an occasional rickshaw jogs past to remind the visitor that this is Kashmir. Moored on the opposite shore are houseboats with English names that ring of misadventure, like *Highland Queen Sanitary Fitted* or *Pride of Kashmir Super Deluxe*. The Kashmiri propel the *shikaras* with heart-shaped oars that are like toys until, sometimes, the craft becomes snarled in undergrowth and poles are brought out to punt the *shikaras* clear. At odd times the men leave off rowing to prepare tea over open coals which smolder at the stern of the boat.

Among the houseboats, on thick floating mats of weeds and roots, there are gardens full of cucumbers, tomatoes, melons and water melons. There are stark poplars and weeping willows, fresh green, silver and shining, all along the shores, and flowers, and apple and cherry blossoms. Some of the *shikaras* that ply the waterways, rocking less gently, are merchant vessels. They are heavily laden with bracelets and earrings, filigree neck-

99

Kashmiri Kashmir

Intricately carved wood paneling adorns the interior of these houseboats — home to hundreds of Kashmiri living beside their floating gardens.

In the Vale, cradled by vast mountains, this freshwater lake (a rarity in Asia) is the focus of human life and ingenuity, which breeds culture.

laces, *papier-mâché* vases and boxes, embroidered woolen shawls made of that famous cashmere wool which comes from the underside of Kashmir's goats. On some of the houseboats beside the lake, where children are loudly selling vegetables from their own *shikaras*, elderly English people sun themselves on the deck verandas. Swans and kingfishers dive into the water, plunging their long necks to catch the scraps. On the verandas there are silver tea services, crumpets and scones. For the expatriate English people, ageing memsahibs, who have settled with a retinue of houseboys, the bright red of the British Empire has hardly faded. Some things have changed — though in things that count for them, much is the same. Perhaps they only mourn the passing of friends.

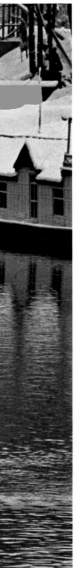

In winter the Valley of Kashmir may be completely cut off from the rest of the world for two or three weeks at a time. Sudden, treacherous landslides make the road across to the Indian plain impassable. When there are storms, which fill unpredictable Kashmiri days, the rain shrouds banks of flowers, airplanes are grounded and telephone wires go dead. On the stranded houseboats there is talk of the tranquility and religious harmony that existed in Kashmir of the Raj. Today, it is murmured, there is an explosive mixture of religion and politics in the Kashmir of independent India. Some say that despite the romance and beauty of the Valley and the mountain ponies climbing twisting, snow-crusted trails to the hill-cottages and pines of the high mountain villages, the fun has left Kashmir. They say the people are jittery and act as though they were being watched. It is also said that India can only remain in Kashmir because the Kashmir government has turned the country into a police state. Then there follows a discussion on the sad history of Kashmir, now called the state of Jammu and Kashmir, and divided since the partition of India in 1947.

Jammu is a Hindu area south of the Valley of Kashmir. But the valley is the heart of the state. It is formed by the Jhelum river and surrounded by mountains of the Karakoram and Himalaya ranges. In 1947, when the partition of India brought the separate Islamic nation of Pakistan into being, princely states throughout the continent had to decide whether to join Pakistan or India. Most Hindu states turned to India while the Islamic ones turned to Pakistan. But the state of Jammu and Kashmir was ruled by a Hindu maharaja, although the majority of the people were Muslims. Pakistani infiltrators tried to take the Valley of Kashmir by force, so the maharaja appealed to India for help. In return he agreed to accede his country to India – Hindu India. This started the first war between India and Pakistan which was ended by a United Nations cease-fire agreement that left the north-western third of the state in Pakistan and the rest with India.

For many hundreds of years the Valley of Kashmir has been famed for its beauty. The Moguls, who overwhelmed most of India during the Middle Ages, loved Kashmir dearly. They laid beautiful gardens and drank from the Chashma Shahi, the Kingly Spring, in the city of Srinagar. One of the great Mogul emperors is often credited with a famous Persian epigram about Kashmir: 'If indeed there be heaven on the face of earth' he said 'it is here, it is here, here it is!' The Valley of Kashmir, 85 miles long and 25 miles broad is, with its mountain glaciers, caverns, quiet dales and dazzling waterfalls, and its springs and streams and lakes, rich in all the natural beauty of a paradise. And the mountains which enclose the Valley have usually tended to preserve successfully its isolation and protect it against foreign invasion. But for the people of Kashmir (and today there are almost two million of them) the mountains have never been

quite enough of a barrier. The lot of the common people was a hard one, whether under the Hindus or Muslims who entered their country. In more recent times the Kashmiri were oppressed successively by the Afghans and the Sikhs and did not enjoy a good administration until late in the 19th century.

After India, the Valley of Kashmir is coolness and color. There are yellow mustard fields, snow-capped mountains and a milky blue sky in which clouds play out real dramas. Kashmiri men are wrapped in brown blankets against the morning mist; barefooted shepherd boys, with caps and covered ears, huddle on the steep rocky slopes. In the villages, dusty in the sunlight, the disorderly bazaars are filled early on with crowds and the air has clinging smells of charcoal and tobacco, cooking-oil and ancient dirt. Grass grows on the mud-packed roofs of cottages and buses rattle past, or halt and are quickly surrounded by small boys begging coins.

The mountains fall back a little as the Valley widens into soft well-watered fields. Roads are lined with poplars and willows drooping to the banks of small streams. In places the villages with their sagging, wood-framed cottages give way to grey stone ruins, centuries old. The 101

Papier mâché artist Jaffar Ali smokes a hookah. The secret of the lacquer technique on the papier mâché table was brought from Persia by his grandfather.

Shikaras, flat bottomed skiffs, cross Lake Dal to the Friday market at Hazratbal carrying vegetables and, in the clear summer, masses of flowers.

massive solid square pillars on a portico, steep stone pediments on a colonnade around a central shrine go back to times of ancient worship. Often they are Hindu ruins, more than a thousand years old, but ignored by the Kashmiri who are mostly Muslims. In the crowded buses that pass these relics no-one points and no-one exclaims their antiquity. Kashmiri can casually bury events of a few hundred years ago as unimportant. They may also assess events which have a doubtful bearing on the present as venerable. In Srinagar, a medieval town, the people are surrounded by wonders: the gardens, pavilions and fountains. But the builders have receded beyond history into legend. A Kashmiri, waving towards the Mogul emperor Akbar's 16th century fort in Dal lake, might say 'That is five thousand years old', and he will not believe otherwise.

The past in Kashmir, at least that part of it which does not fit in with the present, is not considered important. This is especially true of the religious history which has taken many turns. The forms of religious belief for the Kashmiri have not developed over centuries. They have been imposed whole and suddenly by foreign conquerors, displacing other religious forms which once, no doubt, were thought equally unalterable. Few traces of earlier beliefs exist except in the ruins. So complete a conversion is only possible without a sense of history. And the Kashmiri will deny history, like their names which are often purely Hindu, in the cause of the present which is Islam and inviolable.

To politics also, the Kashmiri bring their gifts of myth and wonder. Analyses of the Kashmir situation presented outside the country bear little relation to the problem as the Kashmiri see it. Since the partition of India in 1947 Kashmir has been a more or less constant focus of international conflict. India and Pakistan have fought two bitter wars over Kashmir; the USSR and China have been directly involved. The Valley and its flanking mountains to the west have been thickly garrisoned by Indian troops throughout. But for the Kashmiri, this whole tortured passage of history has been a saga of which the perennial hero is their own champion Sheikh Abdullah, Sher-i-Kashmir – Lion of Kashmir.

There are many myths and legends about Kashmir's past in oral and literary traditions. The *Nilamata* is a famous ancient text believed by modern scholars to date back to the 6th and 7th centuries. It recounts that long ago there was a lake cradled in the Himalayas called Satisar or Sati's lake after one of the names of the Brahmanic god Shiva's consort, Sati. This lake was a favorite resort of gods and goddesses, and holy men resided on its banks. The holy men were disturbed in their devotions by the demon Jalodbhava whom Sati herself ultimately had to destroy. Sati changed herself into the common *sharika* (a bird of the starling family) and, picking up a pebble in her beak, dropped it over the demon's hiding place at the bottom of the lake. The

Winter-hardened Kashmiri
travel confidently in the
mountains. They know that the
yeti (the abominable snowman)
exists: many have seen one.

The single hair from the
prophet Mohammed, housed in
the Hazratbal mosque, has
caused riots among the Hindus
ruled by Muslim Kashmiri.

pebble instantly exploded into a hillock that crushed Jalodbhava and his hordes to death. There is a hillock in the north of the city of Srinagar said to be the same pebble which killed Jalodbhava. The Kashmiri call it *Sharika-parbat*, Sharika's hill. To Hindus the hillock is holy and they walk around it as a mark of devotion. The Mogul emperor Akbar built one of his famous forts on top of it.

After Jalodbhava's destruction some legends say that water was drained from the lake by Shiva. Others say the lake was cleared by Vishnu (another Brahmanic god), and still others attribute the feat to the sage Prajapati Kashyapa, whose son Nilanag is believed to be the author of the *Nilamata*. All this happened, it is said, between 2,000 and 3,000 years ago.

The earliest Kashmir kings in fact were Hindus of local dynasties. But in the middle of the 3rd century BC Buddhism was introduced into Kashmir and it later became a center of Buddhist philosophy and practice. But Buddhist kings gave way to Hindu kings once again. Of these the most illustrious was Lalitadiya (697-738 AD). He not only conquered territories to the south but also to the north, in central Asia. One of his great successors was Avantivarman (855-883 AD) and the ruins of Avantivarman's capital stand by the roadside 17 miles south of Srinagar. Then, in the 14th century, the first Muslim dynasty was founded.

The most famous Sultan, indeed the most celebrated Kashmir king, during the medieval era, was Zain-ul-Abidin, even now remembered as the Baud Shah, Great King. During his rule from 1420 to 1470 he reversed the bigoted policies of the preceding 100 years of Muslim rule by making it possible for Hindus and Buddhists to live in safety and honor in his kingdom. He abolished the hated *jazzia*, a tax imposed on non-Muslims. He called a halt to the destruction of Hindu temples, nearly all of which had been destroyed. He showed keen interest in Buddhist and Hindu philosophy and appointed Buddhists and Hindus to high administrative positions. In his magnanimous treatment of his non-Muslim subjects, he was the true precursor of Akbar, the first of the great Moguls, who came a hundred years later.

The Sultanate was followed by the Chak dynasty, whose last king, Yaqub, was defeated by the armies of Akbar in 1586, when Kashmir was annexed to the Mogul empire. About 175 years later the king of Afghanistan, Ahmad Shah Abdali, conquered Kashmir. Afghan rule was the darkest period in the history of Kashmir. The valley was reduced to helpless subjection and the people were terrorized by Afghan viceroys. Hindus inevitably suffered more than Muslims and representatives of the Hindu community requested Ranjit Singh, the Sikh ruler of the Punjab, to annex Kashmir. He conquered it in 1819. Sikh rule, which was little different from Afghan rule except that now Muslims were persecuted instead of Hindus, mercifully quickly 103

A group of farmers who have gone out in their *shikaras* to the haystacks are caught in a snowstorm as it cuts across Lake Dal from the Himalayas.

(Bottom) Huddled in the bows of their *shikara* mother and child wrap up in a *pheran*, the loose robe made of soft 'cashmere' goat's wool.

ended. In 1846 the government forces of the East India Company defeated the Sikhs and forced them to cede their territories to the British. Following this the princely state of Jammu and Kashmir was created.

In all the towns and in about half of the villages in Kashmir, a few Hindus live alongside the Muslims. All the native Hindus of Kashmir are Brahmans, call themselves Bhatta, and are generally known in India as Kashmiri Pandits. Bhatta and Pandit both mean 'scholar' and point to the rich literary and philosophical achievements of the people's ancestors. The Bhatta are divided into two castes, in each of which the members only marry among themselves: *karkun* (civil servants) and *guru* (priests). It would seem that during the first 100 years of Muslim rule, when there were mass conversions, all Buddhists and all Hindus, except some Brahman families, either embraced Islam or escaped from the valley. In Kashmir's loosely structured caste system, in its exposure to Buddhism and in its mass conversion to Islam there are striking resemblances to the history of Bangladesh.

Bhatta and Muslims neither intermarry nor eat together. Bhatta regard all Muslims as polluting, although not equally so. Muslim goatherds, goldsmiths and landowners are less polluting than butchers, leather workers and scavengers. Nevertheless, Bhatta are dependent on

Muslims for all essential services which help them retain

Hungry dogs and scavenging
birds wait eagerly for
entrails as a goat carcass
is butchered on the
shores of Lake Dal.

A woman brushes snow from
the bows of her *shikara*. The
lake villages are quiet in winter
as craftsmen build up their
stock for summer selling.

their own ritual purity. In this respect the social structure of Kashmir is an interesting variant of the Hindu caste system in which all essential services are provided by Hindus themselves.

The Kashmiri are proud of their literary forbears, those renowned philosophers of the ancient period such as the Buddhist Nagarjuna in the 1st century AD, the Brahman Abhinavagupta in the 10th century and the remarkable 12th century historian Kalhana, who all wrote in Sanskrit. A school of Hindu philosophy flourished after the retreat of Buddhism and propounded the doctrine, popularly known as Kashmir Shaivism, of *Trika*, which means a number of triads that include three modes of knowledge.

New literary traditions that developed after the coming of Islam and of Bhatta and Muslim mystics gave utterance to their thoughts in Kashmiri verse and came close in beliefs and outlook. Among the earliest and most famous of these mystics were the Muslim Shaikh Nurud-din and the 14th century Bhatta poetess Lalla who, though a follower of Shaivism, was much influenced by the austere simplicity of Islam. Their sayings are part of the daily speech of Kashmiri in rural areas even now. Kashmiri, influenced by Persian poets, also began to sing both in Persian and in their own language, of the love of man for women. The foundations of modern Kashmiri literature – mainly poetry – were laid then. Muslims also brought music, Afghan and Persian cuisine, and many arts and crafts to Kashmir.

Kashmiri weavers established a world-wide reputation during the Mogul times as master weavers of woolen shawls, as embroiderers and as woodcarvers. The *shah toos*, later also called 'ring shawl', could be passed through a ring, and the *jamavar* looked like a shawl that had been delicately embroidered, though the pattern was in fact woven. Silk was made in Kashmir as early as the 15th century. Carpet weaving was introduced into the valley by Zain-ul-Abidin who brought weavers from Samarkand. Today's highly skilled carpet makers can do anything the Persians can.

Kashmiri seem to have long been in constant touch with other parts of India. The Saraswat Brahman of Maharashtra, Goa and Mysore claim to be descended from Kashmiri, although it is difficult to establish when their ancestors moved out of their native land. Some communities along the foothills of the Himalayas, such as the Khasa in Uttar Pradesh, call part of their traditional lore Kashmiri *vidya* (knowledge). In medieval times many Brahman families escaped from the valley and settled down in various north Indian cities. Some of these self-exiled Kashmiri Pandits as they call themselves, although few speak the Kashmiri language, have played a prominent part in the public affairs of the subcontinent. Among the most illustrious scions of these families was Pandit Jawaharlal Nehru (1889-1964), nationalist leader, world statesman, and the first Prime Minister of India. 105

Naga
Nagaland

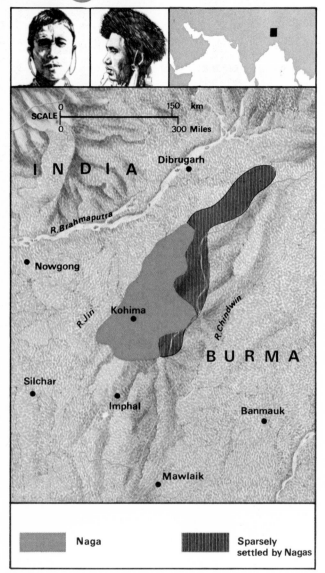

Naga

Sparsely
settled by Nagas

In the mountains along India's north-eastern borders
which enclose the plains of Assam like an enormous
horseshoe live a multitude of tribal populations of
mongoloid race and Tibeto-Burman speech. They differ
fundamentally from the Hindu castes of the lowlands
and have preserved an archaic civilization reminiscent
of the neolithic age. Of these the most numerous and
prominent are the half million Naga of Nagaland who
lived in such long, unbroken isolation from the plainspeople and their historic civilizations that they remained
untouched by Hinduism and Buddhism. Until the beginning of the 20th century when Christianity was brought
by missionaries there was little change in their social
and religious practices.

The ordinary routine of Naga domestic life has so far

remained very similar to what it was a generation ago.
Men and women take an equal share in agricultural
work, sowing and reaping together. The women's household chores of fetching water and firewood and of
pounding rice are unchanged, and the men engage, as of
old, in making baskets and mats, repairing instruments
and periodically rebuilding and rethatching houses. Only
one Naga tribe, the Angami, grow rice on irrigated,
ingeniously constructed terraces. The rest are nearly all
slash-and-burn cultivators of rice, millet, taro and vegetables, who use neither the plow nor draft animals, but
till their fields with small iron hoes.

All Naga dwell in substantial settlements usually on
the highest points of ridges where, in the days of tribal
warfare and headhunting the village could be easily
defended. Their houses are large and well built, with
massive wooden posts, bamboo walls and solid roofs
covered by thick layers of palm leaves. Some houses are
decorated with elaborate carvings indicating the social
achievements of the owner, and many of the hereditary
chiefs of the Konyak Naga live in impressive houses up
to 360 feet long which contain enormous halls lined with
such trophies as the skulls of elephants, buffalo and
other game, quite apart from the rows of captured
enemies' heads which are exhibited as tangible proof of
success in warfare. Even the houses of ordinary villagers
are well built and spacious and give the owner complete
protection against the torrential monsoon rains.

Naga villages are traditionally autonomous, ruled
either by a chief or, more frequently, by a village council.
This council adjudicates disputes, punishes breaches of
the social order, decides matters of ritual and enforces
the observance of the many taboos which the Naga
consider necessary precautions against magical dangers.
After an earthquake or an eclipse of the moon, for
instance, the whole community must abstain for one or
even two days from all activities outside the village. This
is thought helpful in restoring the disturbed balance of
natural forces.

While the social system of most Naga tribes is egalitarian and democratic, others divide society into aristocratic clans and commoners. The aristocrats produce the
chiefs, who have many privileges and wield the arbitrary
power of true autocrats. High rank involves obligations
and, to maintain their eminent positions, Naga chiefs
have to preserve the purity of their noble blood by
marrying within their own class. As well as their principal
wives most chiefs have a number of concubines of commoner status, and the giant houses of prominent chiefs
used to be thronged with a crowd of women and children
of varying status. Commoners have to content themselves with one wife, although premarital affairs are
regarded with great tolerance. The institution of
bachelors' halls and girls' dormitories provides boys and
girls with wide scope for sexual experimentation, and it
is taken for granted that a girl will have several lovers

Isolated in fortified hilltop
villages on India's north
eastern borders, some Naga
tribes were headhunters
as recently as the 1960s.

Naga observe many taboos — a necessary precaution against magical danger. The whole village must stay home after an earthquake or eclipse.

before she marries. Even after the wedding she continues to sleep in the girls' dormitory or her parents' house, and may consort with men other than her husband. It is only after the birth of her first child that she must move into her husband's house and take up her domestic duties. An eldest son is often not the offspring of his mother's husband, who for all social purposes is nevertheless cast in the role of his father. While a man's extra-marital affairs are viewed with indifference as long as they do not break up his marriage, once a wife has entered her husband's house, she is required to remain faithful and infidelities are regarded as breaches of the customary social order.

The bachelors' halls or men's houses serve not only as dormitories for the unmarried, but also as social centers where men of a village-ward assemble for public functions and the performance of religious ceremonies. Many men's houses are decorated with elaborate carvings painted in black, red and white, and contain also the large log-gongs which are beaten on ritual occasions. The members of a men's house share the responsibility of guarding their village-ward against external enemies, and of maintaining the paths to the cultivated land and the forest.

Relations among Naga villages have varied between alliances and hereditary enmities. When headhunting

This Naga woman has complete sexual freedom until the birth of her first child when she must move into her husband's house.

Bands of once mutually hostile tribesmen celebrate Nagaland Republic Day and a new awareness of belonging to one united tribe.

was still rampant – until the 1960s in some parts of Nagaland – it was assumed that outside the group of villages tied to each other by a network of alliances there were hostile villages whose inhabitants would be legitimate victims of raids. Even casual travel outside the village involved risks. People out cultivating distant fields were guarded against marauding enemies by young warriors of their clan and ward. Only inside his village could a man feel secure, for the men of a ward centered on a men's house were a closely-knit group and protected each other.

The custom of headhunting was based on the belief that a part of a man's personality is seated in the skull and remains attached to it even after death. Hence the captor of a head acquires for himself and his village the magical power adhering to the skull of his former enemy, a power which benefits the living by enhancing the fertility of men, animals and crops. The captured skulls are periodically fed with rice and rice-beer, and this ritual practice reflects the belief in the power of a spiritual element remaining on this earth while the dead person's 'soul' has found a new dwelling place in the Land of the Dead, imagined by the Naga to be an exact counterpart of this earth.

As the Naga tribesmen believe that the presence of captured heads in a village magically benefits the whole community, a successful headhunter gained great social prestige and merit. The meritoriousness of his deed lay not in the valor displayed, for valor as such is not valued and the man killed in battle is not accorded the glorification of a hero, but it lay in the concrete achievement of adding to the store of magical power in his village community. The Naga tend to make marks with tallies and symbols to indicate their achievements and success in headhunting entitles a man to wear distinctive ornaments and dress, and among some tribes also to a special tattoo as a mark of his prowess.

The religious beliefs of the various Naga tribes are not uniform. But there is throughout a belief in numerous spirits, which are partly friendly and partly hostile to man, and which can be influenced by rites: animal sacrifices, offerings and invocations. Above a host of earthbound spirits stands the figure of a supreme deity associated with the sky. Some Naga attribute the creation of the firmament to this deity and believe that he causes the thunder to roll and the lightning to flash. At most important events in the life of a Naga the sky god is invoked, and in prayers he is asked to bestow blessings and success on individuals or on the whole community. The Konyak Naga regard the sky god also as the guardian of the moral order. The Naga believe that he can see and hear everything human beings do, and that he is angered by certain offenses against the ethical code. He is invoked by people who have been harmed by unknown wrongdoers, and there is the conviction that such prayers for retribution will be answered, and that supernatural sanctions will be brought to bear on the culprit to bring about his downfall.

The belief in a divine guardian of individual conduct does not amount to the acceptance of a universal morality. None of the moral rules and checks on violence which regulate relations between kinsmen and co-villagers extend to the interaction between autonomous units. The Naga used to distinguish clearly between members of their own individual community whose interests they were bound to respect, and all those beyond the confines of their group of allied villages to whom they owed no consideration and whom they could slay without offending against any moral rule.

Today this outlook is rapidly fading. More than half the inhabitants of Nagaland profess Christianity, and the constitution of the state provides for a system of regional representation which involves co-operation between men of formerly hostile villages and even across tribal boundaries. The change of attitudes resulting from these innovations is profound, for a population divided into small warring units, separated by the threat of headhunting, is being transformed into a people evolving the consciousness of an ethnic identity which embraces all the tribes of Nagaland.

Brahman and Harijan
Tamilnad

The Tamil, of all the ancient Dravidian peoples of south India, have most stubbornly resisted domination by Hindi speaking Aryans of the north.

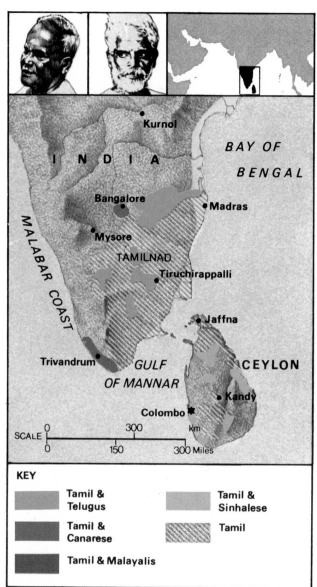

KEY

Tamil & Telugus	Tamil & Sinhalese
Tamil & Canarese	Tamil
Tamil & Malayalis	

Tamilnad, the land of the Tamil, is one of the four states of south India; it has an area of about 50,000 square miles and a population of over 41 million. Tamil, the oldest living language in India, is a Dravidian language and it has a continuous literary tradition about two thousand years old. Tamilnad has a rich and ancient cultural heritage kept alive in its numerous temples, its traditional handicrafts and its classical music and dance. Here too social traditions are more rigidly entrenched, particularly those governing caste.

Tamil society is structurally complex and Brahman and Harijan (or untouchables as the British called them) are at two extremes of their hierarchical caste structure. About four per cent of Tamil society are Brahman. About 18 per cent are Harijan. The differences between 111

Brahman and Harijan Tamilnad

A village grocery is filled with vegetables, spices, curds and lentils — ingredients for the hot spicy curries of the south.

(Bottom) Tamilnad has preserved its most famous dance the *bharata natyam* unchanged for centuries. Dancers wear *koka* ornaments in their pierced noses.

the two groups are not racial or biological. The popular belief that Brahman belong to the Aryan race and Harijan (and other non-Brahman) to the Dravidian race is misleading, although Brahman do tend to be lighter-skinned than most Harijan. What distinguishes them are social and cultural differences. It has been argued that the hierarchy of caste is essentially a ritual hierarchy. Although the ideology of caste is now widely questioned, Brahman by tradition enjoy the highest degree of purity while Harijan are considered to exist in a permanent state of pollution, and in practice the Harijan continue to be associated with the stigma of pollution.

The material conditions in which they live also differ. Brahman have a fairly high economic position – as landowners, priests, teachers, and now increasingly in the modern professions – whereas the Harijan have the lowest economic position. They are either landless agricultural laborers or unskilled workers, sweepers, or scavengers.

In the traditional village the Brahman generally live in a separate street, known as the *agraharam,* where the houses are spacious and made of brick and tiles. The Harijan usually live on the fringe of the village in streets known as *cheris* – strings of huts made of mud and thatch. Harijan were forbidden in the past to enter the *agraharam.* Today they may pass through it, although they usually keep away. The Brahman in their turn do not visit the *cheri* for fear of being ritually polluted. It is generally believed that the Brahman have maintained the purity of their traditional way of life to a greater extent in Tamilnad than in most other parts of the country.

Certainly one can hardly think of any community in the world which has been associated with a continuous tradition of learning for a longer period of time than have the Brahman. Much of their ritual and learning is in Sanskrit, which is very different from Tamil. All Brahman's personal names are of Sanskrit origin, which is not the case among the other castes. When more than a hundred years ago the British introduced a new education system the Brahman were the first to take advantage of it. They used this education as a passport to the new professional, managerial and white-collar occupations. Even today the Brahman are unusually highly represented in the fields of education, law and medicine, and in the higher civil service.

Tamil Brahman are strict vegetarians and required to abstain from alcohol. They will not eat food cooked or served by non-Brahman, and many will eat only in the company of fellow-Brahman.

Tamil Brahman are further divided into three broad categories: temple priests, domestic priests for non-Brahman; and scholars and landowners. Scholars and landowners rank highest, and are subdivided into two castes known as Smartha and Shri Vaishnava. Members of subcastes do not intermarry, and there are strong traditional rivalries between them, each claiming the highest social and ritual position. However recently the

12

Alone in the dawn a Madras peasant makes an early start on the day's work, driving his pair of oxen through the thick mud of the paddy field.

rules of endogamy have become less rigid, so that Brahman are today prepared to marry outside their sub-subcaste—or even their subcaste. Also declining is their preoccupation with ritual purity and Brahman are no longer as strict as they were about their food.

The social inferiority of the Harijan has been more marked in Tamilnad than in most other parts of the country because of the more stringent observance in this state of the rules of purity and pollution. The Harijan continue to suffer from a variety of civic disabilities. They may not, for example, draw water from the wells of other castes. And they may not enter their temples. Although the law now entitles them to worship at the village temple they know that they are not welcome there. It is not only the Brahman who discriminate against them. They are discriminated against by members of all 'clean' castes.

Unlike the Brahman the Harijan eat both fish and meat. They even eat the flesh of animals considered 'unclean' by non-Brahman. Moreover they have for centuries performed the most unclean work – such as scavenging, flaying, and tanning – so that the upper castes might remain ritually clean. They continue to do most of the onerous work in both rural and urban areas, but now more from economic necessity than from religious requirements.

There are several castes and subcastes among the Harijan, principally the Paraiya, the Palla, and the Chakkiliya who often practise a form of untouchability among themselves. Orthodox Palla for instance do not draw water from Paraiya wells. Nor do they allow Paraiya to draw from theirs.

The position of the Harijan has improved, particularly since India became independent in 1947, and the practice of untouchability is now a punishable offense. The government has adopted a policy of 'protective discrimination' giving special benefits, concessions, and scholarships to the Harijan. Seats in elective bodies, including the state legislature and the national parliament, and jobs in government, including the highest cadre of the civil service, are now reserved for the Harijan in proportion to their strength in the population as a whole.

As a result there are now educated Harijan including doctors, lawyers, teachers and civil servants. But they constitute a very small section of the total Harijan population and even they suffer from various forms, both gross and subtle, of discrimination in the ordinary affairs of life. The vast majority of Harijan in the rural areas – and Tamilnad, like the rest of India, is predominantly rural – remain both illiterate and landless. Changes in ideology or ritual attitude cannot achieve much when unaccompanied by changes in material conditions. But younger Harijan show an increasing inclination to fight for their rights, and some of them are turning to organized politics as a way of improving their own and their community's social condition.

People of Sri Lanka (Ceylon)

From the bright sea Sri Lanka's
coast is like the coast of
paradise. Small fish come in to
feed with the rising tide:
perched above, fishermen wait.

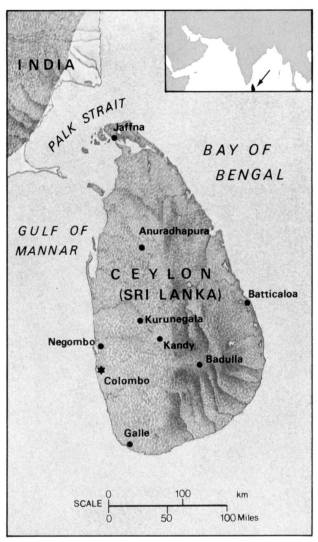

ailors have brought back fantastic travelers' tales of Sri Lanka (Ceylon) for more than 2,000 years. The air was scented with spices they said, especially with cinnamon; the island was rich in jewels – rubies, sapphires and fabulous pearls. Inland there were demon traders and exotic flowers, birds and beasts in the jungle that defied description. Galle on the south-west coast of Ceylon was very likely biblical Tarshish, where Solomon's ships found 'gold and silver, ivory, apes and peacocks'. Marco Polo saw a ruby in Sri Lanka that was 'one palme long and as big as a man's arm'. Chinese merchants made pilgrimages to the great mountain Adam's Peak – where millions of Hindus and Buddhists still make pilgrimages – to see the footprint made by the first man when he lost paradise and came for consolation to Sri Lanka. The Chinese thought Sri Lanka's jewels were this man Pawn-Koo's crystallized tears. Muslim traders called Sri Lanka the island of delight, the Arabs called it Serendip, from

115

People of Sri Lanka (Ceylon)

Stable catamarans are used for
catching big fish like shark
and tunny in deep waters and
high seas. Sri Lanka also
has delicious shell fish.

which the 18th century English writer Horace Walpole coined the word serendipity, which means the art of making happy discoveries. Sri Lanka is staggeringly beautiful, and potentially very fertile. 'No marvel then' wrote Purchas during his 17th century pilgrimage 'if sense and sensualitie have here stumbled on a paradise.'

It was for this wealth, especially for spices, that Moorish, Portuguese, Dutch and finally English adventurers took over all or parts of Ceylon. They were intruding on what had once been a remarkable civilization, though they found only bloody and despotic kings. It was above all a Buddhist civilization, converted to Buddhism in the 3rd century BC by the Indian prince Mahinda. His sister Princess Sanghamitta brought a branch of the sacred bo tree under which the Buddha reached enlightenment, and she planted a shoot at Anuradhapura, which became the Holy City. Twenty-two centuries later it is still growing, in the ruins of the Holy City, casting shadows in the temple courtyard on lotus blossoms and sleeping dogs, its frail branches on iron supports behind golden railings. Buddhism, like the bo tree, is still strong in Sri Lanka, though it has lost sway in India and has here become mixed with Hinduism and other beliefs over the centuries. During the Great Dynasty beginning in the 5th century BC Sinhalese kings made the drought-stricken forest into fertile farm land

and rice fields and gardens, by a complex and very impressive irrigation system of canals and great water tanks. After Mahinda the Sinhalese built huge bell-shaped *dagabas*, housing relics of the Buddha. The oldest agricultural monument still existing in India or Sri Lanka is the Abhayagiriya *dagaba* built in the 1st century BC.

The Sinhalese originally came from North India, and colonized Sri Lanka about 2,500 years ago, fearless of the Vedda, both Yakka – or demons – and Naga, which means snakes. The Vedda (see pages 128–129) were probably indigenous peoples of south Indian or Tamil origin. Yakko means wild man in Sri Lanka today, and until fairly recently there were Vedda living very simply in the forests, eating fruits and honey and not knowing other peoples. There were also many Vedda who, like the Ainu of Japan, were prepared to put on a wild 'Vedda' act for visitors, if paid enough. There are some living in the eastern forests today.

Over the centuries the Sinhalese have divided into two groups: lowland peoples and upland peoples of the Kandyan kingdoms in central and southern Sri Lanka. Altogether there are 7.5 million Sinhalese, named after an ancient king called Sinha which means lion. They form 71 per cent of the total population of 10·5 million. Almost all Sinhalese are Hinayana Buddhists. Most of

A fisherman at Negombo. On the west coast Sinhalese may well be Catholics, and possibly have Portuguese blood. People with Dutch blood are 'Burghers'.

(Bottom) When the boats or the nets are in, fish are taken to the great fish market in the capital, Colombo, named after the explorer Columbus.

(Over page) Fishermen's houses among palms at Galle, which was Old Testament Tarshish, where Solomon's ships came for gold, ivory, apes and peacocks.

the rest are Christians. All speak Sinhalese, an Indo-European language derived from Sanskrit. Sinhalese is now the official language for all Sri Lanka, replacing English.

All Sinhalese have intermarried with various invaders. The Kandyans believe that they have done so less, and can trace their ancestry to the highland families who proudly and ferociously resisted both Tamil and European invaders. Kandyans tend to feel that their culture is purer than that of the lowland Sinhalese. They are more conservative and probably have more Vedda and Dravidian blood. Kandyan law, until recent conformity, was different and based on Roman-Dutch law. Caste organization is probably stronger among the hill peoples, and they are less receptive to industrial and social change than the lowland, often urban, Sinhalese. When, in the 19th century, the British planters wanted workers for their up-country tea plantations they found that the Sinhalese were less prepared to work (or more expensive perhaps) than imported Tamil laborers from southern India.

The Tamil form the second largest ethnic group in Sri Lanka, numbering over 2 million. By now it is difficult to distinguish them by appearance from the Sinhalese, though their skin is darker, their noses are broader and their heads wider. But it is easy to distinguish them by culture, for they are mostly Hindus. About half of them are not Sri Lanka nationals. About half of them technically are foreigners. The Ceylon Tamil are nationals of Sri Lanka. They have lived in the Jaffna Peninsula and the plains of northern Sri Lanka for centuries, since arriving with various colonial conquerors from southern India, and they have established their own culture. They tend to be high caste Hindus, often very highly educated and successful – in fact disproportionately so in the government, the civil service and the professions. Their only ties with southern India are those of language and religion. The 'Indian Tamil' on the other hand are recent low caste immigrants from southern India, or descendants of immigrants after 1830, and many of them are still aliens. Governments trying to control the alarming population explosion have refused to naturalize them, and India will not repatriate them for similar reasons. The Tamil speak a Dravidian language with a script different from Sinhalese script.

Tamil and Sinhalese feel a bitter rivalry for all kinds of reasons. Clearly the Sinhalese are afraid both of displaced Indian Tamil and the cost of supporting them and their many children, and of successful, hard-working Ceylon Tamil. On the other hand, as Sinhalese is the official language and Buddhism is the majority religion, Tamil are at a disadvantage. Some of these tensions lay behind the bloody riots of 1958.

The Moors or Muslims form over 6 per cent of the population. They are descendants of Arabs who dominated the spice trade from the 8th century until the

People of Sri Lanka (Ceylon)

Painted 2,500 years ago at Sigiriya, these women were perhaps courtesans in the eagles' eyries palace built by the parricide King Kassapa.

(Center) The Buddha lies meditating in stone at Gal Vihare in the city of Polanaruwa, which rivals Anuradhapura with its great religious buildings.

(Right) A Hindu ascetic hangs, indifferent to pain, in the lotus pose from hooks through the skin of his calves, with a skewer through his tongue.

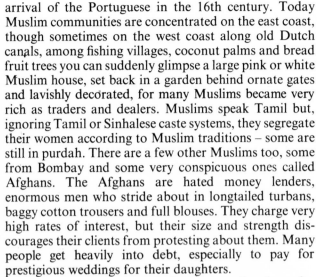

A gathering of *bikkhus* or monks. Buddhism is very fervent in Sri Lanka, and the monks have both direct and indirect influence on public life.

arrival of the Portuguese in the 16th century. Today Muslim communities are concentrated on the east coast, though sometimes on the west coast along old Dutch canals, among fishing villages, coconut palms and bread fruit trees you can suddenly glimpse a large pink or white Muslim house, set back in a garden behind ornate gates and lavishly decorated, for many Muslims became very rich as traders and dealers. Muslims speak Tamil but, ignoring Tamil or Sinhalese caste systems, they segregate their women according to Muslim traditions – some are still in purdah. There are a few other Muslims too, some from Bombay and some very conspicuous ones called Afghans. The Afghans are hated money lenders, enormous men who stride about in longtailed turbans, baggy cotton trousers and full blouses. They charge very high rates of interest, but their size and strength discourages their clients from protesting about them. Many people get heavily into debt, especially to pay for prestigious weddings for their daughters.

There are many other ethnic groups – Burghers, for example, who are descended from the Dutch and who consider themselves European. They are part of the 'trousered class', highly educated and westernized. Even in the 1970s, despite relaxed views about class, caste and race among educated people it is remarkable when a Burgher marries a Sinhalese. The Burghers, whose high position in professions and the civil service has been undermined by government policy, are rapidly emigrating. The Vedda, descendants of aboriginal tribes, are absorbed or very rare. There are Europeans, Eurasians, Chinese, and Kaffirs who were originally imported as slaves. The population explosion, the huge numbers of different ethnic groups and serious financial problems make Ceylon potentially very explosive. More than 10 million live in a country the size of Ireland.

It is difficult for Europeans to discuss it with them though. The Sinhalese live in a caste system, more or less; the system is weakening, especially in towns and it is purely secular – not religious like the Tamil Hindu caste system – but it persists. The more remote a community, the more likely it is to adhere to caste laws and taboos. There are about twenty-five Sinhalese castes of which the cultivators are the highest – for Sri Lanka has depended on rice for centuries and the Sinhalese eat rice at every meal. Cinnamon peelers and toddy tappers rank high. Some cultivators have gone into the urban westernized trouser class, outside the caste system. Smiths, potters, painters and sculptors rank together, slightly lower. The fishermen are in a curious position. Some believe that they are descendants of the Indian warrior caste, one of the Twice-born, and so rank higher than any other Sinhalese caste. On the other hand they take life, by killing fish, which is against Buddhist principles, so they rank low. The Sinhalese used to have untouchables too. The Rodi caste used to live as beggars, scavengers, mountebanks and prostitutes. It is believed

People of Sri Lanka (Ceylon)

The Perahera in Kandy is a sumptuous procession in honor of the Buddha with lavishly decorated elephants carrying symbols of the Buddha's tooth.

As well as jewels and silks elephants at the Perahera wear electric light bulbs for added splendor, attached to batteries on their bellies.

that they were once a noble caste of king's huntsmen. But because a lazy hunter once served human flesh instead of venison to the king they were degraded. Later kings – and some Sinhalese kings were peculiarly despotic – gave the wives and daughters of high-caste people who offended them to the Rodiya. The Rodi women were famous for their beauty and proud bearing – inherited from these reluctant ancestresses perhaps. They used to have to go naked above the waist, so there were postcards of bare bosomed Rodiya girls for sale in the ports of Colombo and Trincomalee.

There is also an important caste of tom-tom beaters, who provide frenzied drummings at the many festivals and ceremonies of the Buddhist year. Every night ominous and mysterious drummings come from the temple. It can be frightening, especially in the hill country in Kandy where black clouds of great crows caw ceaselessly at dusk. The hills round the town seem menacing in the dark and have a strange effect on the noise of the drums.

Ceremonies in the Temple of the Buddha's tooth at Kandy are mesmerizing. The lightness and grace with which people bring lotus blossoms and frangipani to Buddhist shrines seems to be replaced by something darker. And Kandyan temple dancing is frenzied too. Despite their grace and dignified courtesy, the Sinhalese are very passionate and violent and their murder rate is one of the highest in the world. Kandyan temple dancing is insistent and quick, with drumming feet. The dancers are almost weighed down by finely worked silver head-dresses, earrings, heavy belts and jeweled breast plates. Their jewels and eyes gleam almost fiercely, their fingers flash. Like Indian classical dancing, Kandyan dancing is very old indeed and embodies codes of meaning or, more simply, stories. Each gesture, each movement of the eyeball, is controlled to express a meaning. The fastest and most demanding dances are done by men. The women, as in everyday life, take second place and move with extreme grace.

The Kandyan Perahera, or ritual procession in honor of the Buddha, is also very dramatic. Richly caparisoned elephants carry caskets symbolizing the one that held the Buddha's tooth. In fact the Portuguese ground it to dust, but it is supposed to have reassembled itself miraculously.

Life is dominated by religious observance and supporting the monks, or *bikkhu*, who as in all Buddhist countries carry bowls for contributions to their needs. They are to be seen everywhere, stately figures in saffron with huge black umbrellas, which they use as sunshades. (For Tamil estate workers these same umbrellas are a sign of responsibility and status, and they wear them hanging down their backs from their collars.) Monks make daily visits to families and give advice as well as meditating and running temple affairs. Monks take in young novices and in some temples the guide is often a

123

(Above) An elephant bathes in the river in Kandy after work. Sri Lanka elephants are of the Sumatran type, and, oddly, are not related to the Indian type.

Elephants are used for timber hauling and general work, but there are fewer and fewer every year. They also earn money as tourist attractions.

prospective *bikkhu* of only 12 or 13, who solemnly and hospitably shows both Buddhist and Hindu statues sharing the same place. This is so at Isurumuniya, a small rock temple at Anaradhapura where grotesque brightly colored Hindu deities stare out beside placid Buddhist effigies. Isurumuniya has the atmosphere of great antiquity and tranquility that is so common in Ceylon. It has the magic of India without the continual disturbing sight of desperate poverty. Though there is poverty in Sri Lanka, you never see – except perhaps in Colombo and one or two other cities – beggars who are visibly very ill or dying.

Sri Lanka is a poor country. Her main exports were until recently tea, rubber and coconut products. Tourism, with its mixed blessings, is now being developed into a main industry because the rubber trade has been under-cut by world synthetics industries. Though coconut is a food crop, tea is mainly a cash crop and Sri Lanka has to import well over half its staple food, which is rice. Most industries have been nationalized, and the government is continually trying to reclaim land for cultivation. The educational system started by the British has been successfully developed and the Sinhalese have very high educational standards. But Sri Lanka's problems are alarming.

British planters introduced tea and rubber in the hill country. The tea estates often look strange anachronisms. Planters' houses in English styles stand in English gardens which used to grow roses and velvet lawns. Inside tea factories, in the tasting rooms, there are often old photographs of early 20th century planters' tea parties or cricket parties with everyone dressed formally in white – a little piece of England exported to the heat and isolation of up-country Sri Lanka. The factories themselves are continually being modernized, but for the Tamil workers the days of picking and planting and weeding haven't changed very much.

Many other industries have remained even more traditional than the tea industry, especially as most Sinhalese live in the country. Rice growing is one. Paddy fields with oxen drawing hand plows are a common sight. Batik making is another occupation that has changed little. Batik is a craft of Malay origin, a special way of waxing cloth and dyeing pictures and designs onto it. Sinhalese designs are distinctive, using the symbols and stories of their rich traditions or motifs from the astonishing variety of animals, like the Holy Cobra, the lion or the elephant. There is a geological theory that Sri Lanka was once in a huge land mass linked to Madagascar, and Ceylon has some Madagascan species, like the sloth whose tears are used as love philters. In any case, Sri Lanka's natural wealth is more remarkable even than Madagascar's. It is often among the trees and animals that batik is made. In a breadfruit clearing, dyes are mixed in the stumps of breadfruit trees, and under a palm awning sit circles of little girls, around vats of wax, into which they dip

124

The graceful ease of the palms of the south-west are likened to the Sinhalese, just as the sturdy Jaffna trees resemble the Jaffna Tamil character.

Tamil women pick tea, choosing only the best leaves, on an up-country estate. For them plantation work has changed little since colonial times.

brushes to paint designs onto the cloth. When the cloth hangs out to dry the girls scare away insects against a background of raucous birdsong from the forest.

Coastal fishing is largely traditional. The men often use swift outriggers – though modern motorized craft are also used. It is quite common to see large groups of fishermen in bright sarongs hauling in great nets from the sea full of seir or whiting. In some places the fishermen wade into deep water, and stick stilts onto the sea bed. They sit on them for hours above the surface of the water, looking like predatory birds, one-legged herons waiting patiently in the blazing blue water beside flawless beaches. Along the west coast they have a network of Portuguese or Dutch canals which they use as transport to the city from their shady villages under the palm trees.

Digging for jewels is done in the old way too. Sinhalese and Tamil consult astrologers for an auspicious day, and time to dig. Most important decisions are influenced by astrology. If a marriage broker discovered that two young clients were astrologically incompatible he would not further the match. At a propitious time the gem diggers excavate in the simplest ways, using sieves. Some grow one finger nail into a long claw to help them dig and sift. They find both precious and semi-precious stones. The beautiful milky moonstone is so common

there as to be of little value. The government takes its due and the stones find their way into dark intimate dealers' shops in Kandy or Colombo where merchants scatter handfuls of rubies and sapphires onto cushions of black velvet. The same jewelers deal in intricate worked silver, or silver gilt, made into elaborate forms which are often Arab designs. Jewels have been sold this way since the Kublai Khan was refused the ruby Marco Polo saw.

Other Ceylonese skills like woodcarving are being used in the tourist industry. Inlaid woods, elephants and leopards carved from ebony, worked ivory and ritual masks from southern Ceylon are gathered to a central market in Colombo, and sold at state registered prices.

Textiles are an important cottage industry. As well as batik, the Sinhalese make finest silks and cotton in humming bird, flamingo and butterfly colors, sometimes threaded with gold. These are usually sold in sari or sarong lengths, to be worn at festivals or celebrations draped like Indian saris. Sometimes they make transparent veils for women to put over their heads and shoulders in the evening when the heat of the day gives way to a sharp chill.

Traditional services are being offered to tourists as well. Snake charmers visit every hotel. They are scantily dressed and low-caste and it is often difficult to tell 125

People of Sri Lanka (Ceylon)

Women wearing flowers and their best saris crowd together at a feast during the Buddhist Vel Festival in the busy streets of Colombo.

The narrow streets of Kandy, smelling of spices and street vendors' cooking, lead to avenues of sweet-smelling trees round the artificial lake.

whether the snake or the charmer looks more surly. Astrologers offer their services to tourists, though they are rarely more inspiring than the horoscopes at home. Basket makers and potters will make things to order and will often let you watch. Even the hour when elephants go to bathe in the river after their work hauling timber in the jungle, has become profitable. At Kandy visitors are encouraged to ride the elephants, who wait impatiently for the sluggish cool of the river. The elephant owners then charge very high prices for a minute's ride. Similarly, tiny children loiter at temples pressing expensive lotus blossoms on tourists and listing all their tragic misfortunes in the sing-song voice child beggars have in Saigon.

The coconut industry was believed by censorious planters to suit the indolent Ceylonese because it requires little cultivation. The tree is said to love people, thriving best near humans, but this is probably because it does well on human waste and sewage. The Ceylonese used to say that with fine coconut trees, a breadfruit tree, a water buffalo and a right to part of a rice field, no one could want more. The coconut tree provides for a huge number of needs. The tree is graceful and feathery and never grows straight. It blossoms every three months, providing frequent crops, producing food, drink, rope mats, fences, roofing, firewood and oil for light and cooking. About 140 coconuts a year are eaten in Ceylon for every man, woman and child on the island. No one need starve when living near a coconut tree. The meat of the nut, scraped into a cream, is used in curries. The leaves make pickles and preserves. The immature nut produces medicine and sweets. And the mature nut gives sweet milk and flesh. The sap becomes toddy or, when distilled, arrack which with betel is an important part of every Ceylonese man's diet. For export copra, coconut oil and desiccated coconut are produced, as well as coir for rope, hats and so on. Most village houses are built and roofed with coconut substances. But despite its use and versatility the coconut brings in only a tiny percentage of Ceylon's gross national income.

Devil dances were once a
serious method of driving
evil spirits from sick people.
Now they are performed
as popular entertainment.

127

Vedda
Sri Lanka (Ceylon)

The Vedda, a semi-nomadic tribe inhabiting the forests of the highlands of central Ceylon, are the most archaic people in Asia. They are one of the remnants of a primitive racial stratum which, in prehistoric times, extended over large parts of south and south-east Asia. They are small in stature, with dark brown skin and curly or wavy hair. They have broad faces with flat noses, deeply set eyes, very full lips and weak and often receding chins. As the Vedda were the first people of this type to be studied by anthropologists, they have given their name to the entire racial group now known as Veddoids. Many of the primitive jungle-tribes of southern India belong to this group and resemble the Vedda of Ceylon, not only in physical appearance but also in their way of life and general level of culture. Under the pressure of materially more developed populations these tribes, like the Vedda, gradually receded into inhospitable mountains and dense forests, and only in such refuge areas do they exist still in compact groups.

These nomadic foodgatherers and hunters of south Asia have perpetuated a way of life typical of the early stone age and in Ceylon the link between the remote past and the present day is still in evidence. In caves still recently inhabited by Vedda stone implements of palaeolithic type have been found, and there can be little doubt that these arrow points, flakes and scrapers were the products of the predecessors, if not the direct ancestors, of the present-day Vedda.

Today the Vedda are fast losing their tribal identity. It is only a question of time before they will eventually be submerged by the Sinhalese peasantry. They no longer lead the life of nomadic hunters and food-gatherers, but practise a primitive type of shifting cultivation or work as agricultural laborers in the employment of more advanced populations.

Even at the beginning of the 20th century some sections of the tribe had already completed the transition to a settled form of life. But at that time there were still some bands of Vedda who persisted in their old ways. They lived exclusively on wild tubers, jungle fruits, honey and the meat of the game which they killed with bow and arrow. They used wooden digging sticks to unearth edible roots, a task which was shared by men and women. They roasted all their food on a spit or in the ashes of a fire, but never boiled it in water. The honey of rockbees, which was a very important part of their diet, they collected by means of frail rope ladders suspended from trees above the cliffs, cutting off the honeycombs with a sort of wooden sword. Although they were keen hunters and experienced in the use of

(Top) The Vedda are but a tiny remnant of a primitive race which, in prehistoric times, was spread over vast stretches of Asia.

Only one generation has passed since cave-dwelling Vedda were making and using stone-age tools like scrapers and arrow heads.

Today the Vedda have almost disappeared as a tribe. Many have given up their nomadic hunting and gathering to work for the Sinhalese as laborers.

dogs they had devised no methods for trapping game or birds, an ignorance of traps and snares which they shared with the more primitive of the south Indian forest tribes. They caught fish by poisoning the water of pools or shooting them with arrows.

The Vedda changed their camps as seasons and food supply demanded, and they either made ample use of the caves which proliferate in their homeland, erected temporary shelters of a slanting roof made from leafy branches, or camped in the shade of trees. The average Vedda community was of three to five families who shared hunting rights and property rights over a tract of land. There is the tradition that in the old times intruders into another group's territory might be killed by its rightful owners. A married man, however, had free access to the hunting grounds of his wife's people, and spent much of his time with his wife's kinfolk.

All Vedda are organized in clans in which descent runs in the female line. The most preferred marriages are, as well as being monogamous, between the children of a brother and a sister.

Although the Vedda have for centuries lived close to Buddhists they retain their own tribal religion. Most of their ritual practices relate to the cult of a multitude of deities and spirits believed to be capable of helping or harming human beings. Closest to man are the 'new spirits', the spirits of the departed. Men who possess the gift of inducing a state of trance are credited with the power to establish contact with the spirits, who are accessible to prayers and offerings and who, if suitably propitiated, will do the bidding of their worshippers. The Vedda traditionally worshipped gods and spirits to gain their assistance in hunting and honey collecting. Since they have taken to agriculture they now tender their offerings of honey and rice to win the spirits' protection over the crops. Vedda priests occasionally act as oracles and become the mouthpiece of the spirits.

The spirits of the dead are thought to watch over the moral conduct of the living. Any expression of anger towards one's fellow men offends the spirits, as do any acts of violence, including, for example, even hitting a dog. While the spirits do not inflict supernatural sanctions on adulterers or thieves, offended parties can appeal to the spirits and solicit their intervention. Social relations do not end with death. A man's friends are thought to help him when they have become spirits. The Vedda believe that children who die under the age of nine or ten do not become spirits, but are born again.

Relations between the Vedda, as lords of the forest, and Sinhalese villagers can be traced to the remote past. Many myths and legends tell of Buddhist princes who had Vedda wives. Even some of the divine figures of folk religion are believed to have had Vedda mistresses in addition to their official consorts. At one time Vedda may have been relatively more important in Ceylonese life than when first encountered by western observers. 129

Prehistory of India

The Indian subcontinent – today's India, Pakistan, Sri Lanka and Bangladesh – is a clearly defined geographical entity. It is separated from the adjacent parts of Asia by massive mountain ranges, and from the rest of the world by seas. Within the subcontinent there exists almost every type of tropical or near-tropical climate, from arid desert to dense forest. This has produced a wide variety of human cultures.

The early and middle Stone Ages of India (Lower and Middle Palaeolithic) parallel those of western Asia, Europe and Africa, and span hundreds of thousands of years and several major fluctuations of climate. The tools of the early Stone Age most commonly found are hand-axes made from flakes of quartzite. The middle Stone Age tools are generally smaller, finer, and vary more from region to region. No human skeletal remains have so far been found with the tools of either period. The people of that time do not seem to have inhabited caves where layers of débris might have been found, so we know little of their way of life.

Upper Palaeolithic sites have been found only in central Gujarat, eastern Rajasthan, southern Uttar Pradesh, and parts of Andhra Pradesh. During the Upper Palaeolithic period, beginning well over 100,000 years ago, men developed a technique of making parallel-sided stone blades, burins (engraving tools) and other implements of which planes, chisels, saws and adzes are the metal counterparts. The same technique was used in all subsequent Indian cultures until the beginning of the Iron Age some two thousand years ago. It is still used by bead-makers working in agate and other semi-precious stones.

Parallel-sided stone blades are an important element in the more recent Mesolithic cultures which developed in almost every province of the subcontinent from at least 12,000 years ago. Because they tend to be small, the stone tools of this period are often referred to as microliths. Now, at last, we have more than stone tools with which to attempt to reconstruct the cultures of the past. We can say with reasonable confidence that the Mesolithic peoples of India are the direct ancestors of many tribal groups still living in remoter parts, and recorded during the past century. Among such groups we may cite the Chenchu in eastern Andhra Pradesh and the Vedda of Sri Lanka. Mesolithic people inhabited rock shelters wherever they were available, and these provide a fuller record for the archaeologist in the layers of débris which accumulated on the floor. Some of these same rock shelters are still inhabited after thousands of years. Some are decorated with rock paintings or chalk drawings. Mesolithic people also camped in the open, generally on hillocks or rising ground. Where particularly suitable stones for tool-making were lying around, they created large factory sites. At some Mesolithic sites human bones have recently been found. The sizes of these bones, and particularly the different shapes of the skulls, suggest that there were a wide range of physical types.

The Mesolithic was the age of hunting, gathering, and fishing, and the bow and arrow almost certainly came into use at this time. Most of the wild animals in India today, including several species of antelope and deer, pig, rhinoceros, buffalo and porcupine, were then hunted for food. The bones of sheep, goats, and cattle have also been found at some sites dating from the fifth millennium BC. This suggests that the people were pastoralists as well as hunters.

By 3000 BC men had begun to settle down as farmers in various parts of the subcontinent. In some regions the change to settled life and cultivation appears to have been gradual; in others it came to the people more swiftly as settlers arrived from outside, probably mainly from the north-west, bringing with them the new way of life. In eastern India, Neolithic (late Stone Age) techniques of pottery and stone axe-making point to India's connections with Burma, south China and South-east Asia. This is not true of south India where third millennium Neolithic settlements suggest some western influence – though they appear to be mainly a local development from the existing Mesolithic culture. All these cultures were based more or less upon established settlements, with a mixed – if simple – economy including hunting, herding and small-scale cultivation. They all produced hand-made pottery and stone and bone tools. Each, however, already had a highly developed individual character evident in the siting of each of the settlements – beside rivers, in forests, or on hills or plains – and in their varying crafts and economies. This is the time when the regional cultures of modern south Asia began to take shape, and many of the more primitive agricultural communities still have a pattern of life which probably stems from these local Neolithic cultures.

Around the opening of the third millennium BC settled communities appear to have moved eastwards from Baluchistan and established their homes on the plains by the great Indus river of today's Pakistan. Little is known of the earlier population of this area. In the following centuries these communities developed a more or less uniform material culture that extended from the mouth of the River Indus to the foot-hills of the Himalayas. The fertile soil of the alluvial plains with their annual flooding was easily exploited. The people grew wheat and barley and their cattle grazed in rich pastures. These communities used the plow and made implements of copper as well as stone. Their settlements were surrounded by walls of brick or stone and their houses were built of mud-brick. This is the 'early Indus' or 'pre-Harappan' stage. It leads, quite suddenly, somewhere around 2,300 BC, to the development of city life and to the emergence of the first Indian civilization.

The Indus civilization covered an area more or less comparable with that of modern Pakistan. The change to a more unified culture must have been based on this early Indus culture, but it is quite possible that the immediate spark which set it in train came from the outside, possibly in the shape of new arrivals from the west.

The life of the Indus civilization is known to us mainly from the great city sites of Mohenjo Daro, Harappa and Kalibangan. Few minor settlements or villages have been excavated, and none sufficiently thoroughly to give us any idea of the role of the village at that time. Each of the three cities was carefully planned and built on a north-south axis, with a strongly fortified mound to the west, surrounded by massive walls of brick with square bastions. These 'citadel' mounds appear to have contained buildings of civic and probably ritual importance. These included great storehouses, a still little understood temple complex, the remarkable bath complex of Mohenjo Daro, and a group of mysterious platforms at Kalibangan.

To the east of the citadel lay the main residential area, also surrounded by a wall, and with a well-orientated grid of streets, lanes and houses built of both burnt and mud bricks. They had flat roofs and some probably had upper storeys. A large house would have its own bathrooms with well-laid brick floors, and drains connecting to drains in the road outside. In some cases privies have also been discovered. The kitchens at Kalibangan are reported to have had two types of cooking hearth, one above floor level resembling the modern *chula,* and the other below the floor, resembling a small *tandur* oven. Cemeteries lay outside the city, and in at least one instance a small temple was found at a short distance from the city wall.

Copper, bronze and copper-arsenic alloy were used for tools as well as stone; and lead, silver and gold were also used for special purposes. Minor crafts included the working of shell, ivory and various fine stones to make beads and seals. Cotton textiles were already being produced. Transport was provided by bullock carts, more or less identical with the modern bullock carts of the region, and probably by boats, although little evidence survives. There are traces of widespread internal trade in hand-crafted articles, and of imports of raw materials from many adjacent regions. There are also signs of trade with Mesopotamia. Indus products, particularly beads and inlays, are found in excavation sites of the Babylonian kingdoms which were flourishing at the same time. There is less clear evidence of what was imported into India. Nor do we yet know much about the organization of this trade, but it was regulated by well established weights and measures, and by the use of the yet undeciphered script. The seals seem to have been used in some way for marking merchandise, and possibly for accounting.

It is not yet possible to describe the obviously complex organization and government of a state of such dimensions, nor indeed to say whether there was any single supreme authority. But many things point towards some social or political unification. The same picture symbols recur on seals and other objects from widely separated places suggesting a unified ideology. One can already sense a distinctly Indian character, with animal and tree cults, and a mythology that foreshadows many elements in ancient as well as modern Indian folk religion. Many features of the planning and architecture of these cities still survive in modern towns and villages of Punjab and Sindh.

A series of migrations of Indo-Iranian language speakers into India started in the second millennium BC. It seems probable that the people known to us from their cemeteries in Baluchistan and in the valleys of the far north-west (the so-called Gandhara grave complex) stem from these migratory movements. Quite what relation these migrations have to the end of the Indus civilization remains a mystery. But, for whatever reason, the cities and the whole Indus way of life seem to have come to an abrupt end around 1750 BC.

In the south the old Neolithic culture continued in the second millennium with little sign of change, although objects of copper and bronze become more common, and there are several indications of influence from farther north. In the lower Ganges valley and in eastern India very different cultures flourished, with emphasis on rice cultivation.

The beginning of iron-working in south Asia is generally assumed to have come from the west. Radio-carbon dates now suggest that this happened around 100 BC in the north (far earlier than was once thought) and that iron working spread rapidly thereafter to the south and east. In the Ganges valley and west India the early centuries of the first millennium BC witnessed the emergence of the cities and states of classical Indian civilization, and the beginning of the historical period. Writing, of which there is no evidence after the end of the Indus civilization in 1750 BC, reappears around 700 BC apparently newly developed and inspired by the north Semitic scripts. It soon produced the fine phonetic Brahmi script, the ancestor of later Indian scripts. The cities are marked by great ramparts of brick and earth or stone, and wide moats. It was in one of these cities that the parents of Gautama the Buddha lived in the 6th century BC.

In the south the spread of iron working is associated with a nomadic people known to us principally by their graves. There are several varieties of these graves, which are found in the extreme south and as far north as Nagpur, but they all have features in common. Nearly all involve stone circles · and all have stone cists (or chambers), and for this reason they are called Megalithic. In them, iron objects are frequently found, along with black-and-red burnished pottery. Here, too, towards the end of the millennium we enter the historical period, and in the plains of Tamilnad we encounter the oldest inscriptions in Tamil.

13

India 1500 BC to 20th Century AD
Formative Influences

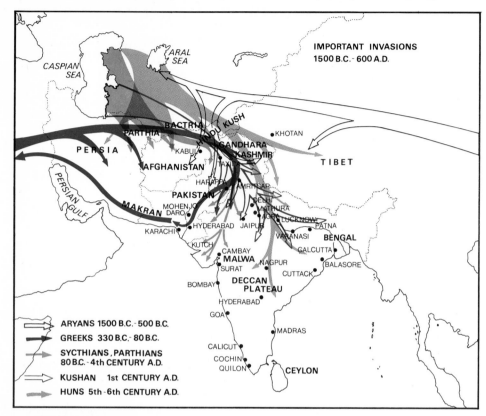

IMPORTANT INVASIONS
1500 B.C. - 600 A.D.

ARYANS 1500 B.C. - 500 B.C.

GREEKS 330 B.C. - 80 B.C.

SYCTHIANS, PARTHIANS
80 B.C. - 4th CENTURY A.D.

KUSHAN 1st CENTURY A.D.

HUNS 5th - 6th CENTURY A.D.

Around 1500 BC Aryans invaded the north-west passes of the Himalayas and conquered the Indus valley. The Aryans were illiterate Bronze Age warrior-herdsmen from the Fertile Crescent, and radically changed the indigenous culture. Although the initial Greek invasion under Alexander the Great in the 4th century BC was resisted by the first of the Mauryan kings, later Greek invasions from Bactria were more successful: Menander ruled kingdoms from Kabul well into the Punjab. Scythians and Parthians, under pressure from Chinese nomads, invaded Bactria and then the lower Indus valley in the 2nd century BC. A similar people, called Kushan by the Indians, was soon forced out of north-west China, settled in Bactria, and in the early 1st century AD conquered land around Kabul and further west. Then came the great Gupta empire which fell in the 6th century AD into barbarians' hands. By 540 AD western India was controlled by Hun kings, who went the farthest south of all the invaders.

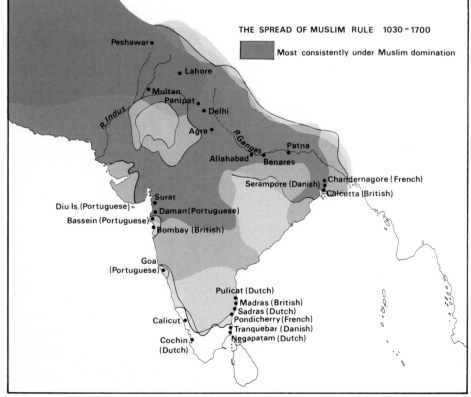

THE SPREAD OF MUSLIM RULE 1030 - 1700

Most consistently under Muslim domination

Islam was brought into India from the north-west, by Muslim Turks of central Asia. Their early raids and holy wars against the disunited Indian non-Muslim infidels developed into a highly organized, far-reaching empire, first based in Delhi in the 13th century. Hindu traditional hatred of Muslims originated from this period. The empire reached greatness in the Mogul period and finally lost control of its territories and subject princes in the 18th century, when it was reduced to a little land round Delhi.

At the beginning of the 20th century territory owned or governed by the British seemed as extensive and secure as ever. But times were changing. The formation in 1885 of the Indian National Congress marked the beginning of the end of British domination. The Congress, at first ignored by the British, became the chief voice of Indian nationalism, and by the 1920s was too extreme to accept the tentative British proposals towards representation and real power for the Indians. Ultimately the Congress became the government of independent India which replaced British rule.

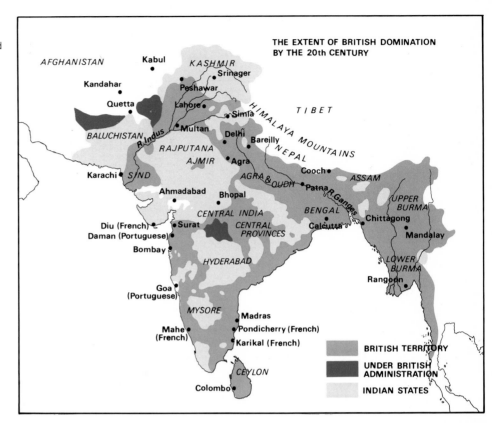

THE EXTENT OF BRITISH DOMINATION BY THE 20th CENTURY

BRITISH TERRITORY

UNDER BRITISH ADMINISTRATION

INDIAN STATES

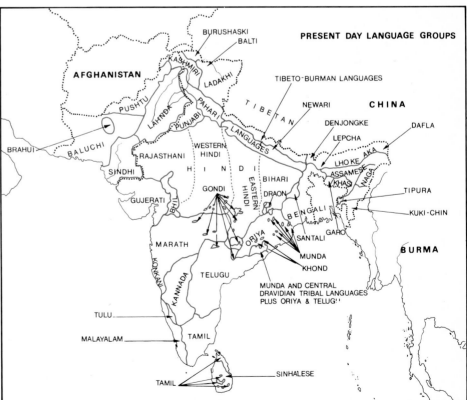

PRESENT DAY LANGUAGE GROUPS

More than 200 languages are spoken in India today. The parent of most of the languages of northern India, which include Hindi, Urdu, Punjabi, Marathi, Bengali and Assamese is Sanskrit, a member of the Indo-Aryan (European) language family. The four main languages spoken south of the Narbada river — Telugu, Tamil, Malayalam and Kannada — are Dravidian and may be related to Finnish and Hungarian. Languages of the Munda group, all of them unwritten, the western branch of the Austro-Asiatic languages, may represent the most ancient surviving language group in India. Tibeto-Burman languages are an extension of a language group centered on Tibet and Burma. As these many languages are often mutually incomprehensible, English is often in practice the *lingua franca*.

13

Glossary to the peoples of the Indian subcontinent

In the Indian sub-continent there are many more distinct tribes than it is possible to include in this glossary, though many Himalayan peoples are included in Volume XIII. Moreover in this area the distinction between tribe and caste is not always clear. For centuries, and it is a continuing process, the main body of the Indian caste structure has been assimilating the tribal people. And many of the lower castes, who may marry only among themselves, have, conversely, the characteristics of a tribe. They may have their own dialect, their own variation of Hinduism, and appear to be racially homogeneous. While some broad groups of the broad sections of the Indian population that have an ethnological entity (eg Rajasthani) are mentioned in the glossary by name, large numbers of Indian nationals do not have specific ethnological identity and are not included.

Few Indian tribes, as in most developing countries, can maintain their isolation from contact with non-tribal society. Change, where it has not already been forced upon the tribal peoples, is imminent. Distinct tribal languages, for example, traditionally a vital element in tribal cohesion, are threatened. Many tribal languages are now dying out. And with new languages people inevitably acquire new ideas and religious beliefs.

The traditional tribal social patterns, religious practices and subsistence economies are all incompatible with modern conditions. Changes brought about by new influences are often enforced by legal pressure. As the traditional tribal slash-and-burn method of cultivation, in which new cultivable land is cleared from the forest and the covering vegetation burnt off, effectively devastates forest areas and erodes the soil, slash-and-burn communities have been forced to settle and not move on whenever they exhaust the soil. With new methods forced upon them tribal peoples must also learn new craft techniques. They have also begun to abandon the traditional barter system as they join a money economy. Where tribal people have been forced by economic pressures to live on the fringe of industrial society, working as laborers, they have also been made to conform to the prevailing, non-tribal morality.

Some larger tribes, particularly when they are the dominant people of an area, have managed to keep their identity while simultaneously absorbing advanced techniques of industrial society and even sometimes while living in towns. Often the effect of exposure to the national education system is to enforce, rather than weaken, their sense of tribal identity and of their tribe's best interests. They become politically active on behalf of their tribe.

In the more inaccessible areas, however, where tribal populations have not increased too much for the available food resources to sustain them, there are people whose way of life has changed little since prehistoric times.

ADI *Population:* 4,000. Language group: Tibeto-Burman. The Adi live in the tract of hills which rise on both sides of the Siang and the Yamne Rivers and extend between the plains of Assam and the Tibetan border. Until some years ago the Adi were known as Abor, a term which has been abandoned because of its derogatory meaning – wild man. The Adi are of a mongoloid physical type. They are divided into several distinct sections of which the Minyong and the Gallong are the best known. They live by growing dry rice, millet and maize by shifting cultivation on the hill-slopes and by raising the *bos frontalis* breed of cattle for meat and sacrifice, as well as pigs and goats. Their large villages of bamboo houses built on wooden piles traditionally have a bachelors' house and girls' dormitories.

ANDAMANESE *Population:* 1,000. Language: Andamanese. The indigenous inhabitants of the Andaman islands south-west of Burma in the Bay of Bengal have never recovered from their devastating contact with European diseases like measles, influenza and syphilis. They are now declining in numbers. These people are of the distinctive negrito race. They are short with dark skins and frizzy hair.

The Andamanese live in clusters of semi-nomadic families who own land in a particular area, led by men and women elders. They shift within their area to recognized camping places or groups of huts inhabited by 30 to 50 people. Each local group generally has a permanent encampment as well as these numerous short-term camps and hunting-camps. Some tribes are exclusively either coast- or forest-dwellers, and identifiable by a coastal or forest means of livelihood. The coast dwellers rely primarily on fishing and turtle hunting with canoes, though they also eat edible roots, fruits and occasionally wild pig from the forest. The forest dwellers, on the other hand, rely solely on the forests and inland creeks for their food supply. They are more skilful than the coast dwellers at pig hunting but are poor fishermen.

ANGLO-INDIANS *Population:* 200,000. Language: English. Anglo-Indians are of mixed European and Indian descent. They have been associated with the development of the Indian telegraph and railway systems, and many are still employed in these services. They are concentrated in the large cities where they live in closed groups, sending their children to special schools. They are Christians and live in European style. They tend not to mix socially with Indians.

APA TANI *Population:* 11,000. Language group: Tibeto-Burman. The Apa Tani live in a single valley in the Subansiri district of Arunachal Pradesh. They cultivate rice intensively on skilfully irrigated fields. They do not use the plow but cultivate their fields by hand with iron hoes. They keep cattle for meat and for sacrifice, but do not milk them. The Apa Tani are enterprising traders and barter rice for livestock and cotton with their Dafla (q.v.) neighbors. Each village, of many hundreds of houses built on piles, is a political unit. The people are divided into an aristocratic class, commoners and slaves – until these were freed in the 1950s when the Apa Tani came under Indian rule. Until the late 1940s the Apa Tani were often at war with tribal neighbors, but today they are peaceful and have developed trading contacts with the Assamese of the Brahmaputra plains.

ASSAMESE *Population:* 15 million.
Languages: Assamese and Bengali. The
Assamese are a mongoloid people, the
eastern branch of the mongoloid peoples
found among the Himalayan foothills from
Kashmir to Assam. They are also related to
the Shan, from the headwaters of the
Irrawaddy river, who began to conquer
Assam at the end of the 8th century. The
Assamese language is an eastern branch of
Bengali, an Indo-Aryan language.

Most Assamese are farmers. Peasant-grown
rice occupies the largest area of land in
Assam but tea is of far greater commercial
importance. Tea plantations employ nearly a
million workers and produce about 55 per
cent of India's total tea crop.

The Assamese are proud of their literature
which developed independently of the rest of
India. Chronicles go back 600 years and
knowledge of their contents is part of the
education of the upper classes. The best
known writer is the 15th century poet, Sankar
Deb. Forty or fifty dramatic works are still
acted some of which date back to the time of
Sankar Deb.

BADAGA *Population:* 70,000. Language
group: Dravidian. The Badaga live in the
Nilgiris hill area of Madras state. They are
highly skilled rice farmers, who succeed in a
harsh environment. Their buffalo are herded
for them by the Toda (q.v.) in exchange for
rice and grain.

BAGATA *Population:* 57,000. Language:
Telugu (Dravidian). The Bagata live in the
thick tropical forests of the Eastern Ghats in
north-eastern Andhra Pradesh. They
occasionally share settlements with other
tribal groups in the area, the Valmiki (q.v.),
the Gadaba (q.v.) and the Samantha (q.v.).
On the hill slopes they grow millet, pulses and
maize by slash-and-burn and small quantities
of rice in streamside plots. In plots beside
their houses they grow sweet potatoes, chilies,
tobacco and varieties of vegetables. They also
eat the fruits of the jack, mango and tamarind
trees. They keep chickens, sheep and goats
and relish the occasional wild boar they are
able to catch.

BAIGA *Population:* 145,000. Language:
Chattisgarhi Hindi (Indo-Aryan). The Baiga
are a primitive tribe who live in small

communities interspersed with Gond (see
pages 72-75) in the forested hills of the
Mandla, Balaghat and Bilaspur districts of
Madhya Pradesh. Originally they were
slash-and-burn cultivators using iron hoes,
but they are beginning to use plows drawn by
bullocks despite their traditional belief
that plowing would offend Mother Earth.
The Baiga also gather wild fruits and roots.
They have the reputation of being expert in
magic, and their priests serve not only their
own community but also neighboring tribes.
They have an elaborate mythology and a rich
oral poetry. A separate area in Mandla
district, known as Baiga Chak, now serves as
a kind of reservation where the Baiga are able
to continue their traditional way of life.

BANJARA see LAMBADA

BENGALI *Population:* 115 million.
Language: Bengali. The Bengali language,
with Bihari, Oriya and Assamese, comprises
the eastern branch of the Indo-Aryan group
of languages. They are a quick-witted,
volatile people, of slight build and brown
skins. They live in Bangladesh and West
Bengal. The name Bengali is derived from the
ancient kingdom on the Ganges known as
Vanga or Banga. Rice is the Bengali's staple
food. It is grown on four fifths of the
cultivated land in west Bengal. Three harvests
are gathered each year. Bengali farmers also
grow large quantities of jute, one of India's
most valuable exports.

Bengali has a long and flourishing literary
history. The earliest work in the Bengali
language is a collection of lyrics written
before the 12th century. The modern literary
Bengali language arose early in the 19th
century under the revival of Sanskrit
learning in Calcutta. Two out of three
Bengali are Muslim, the third is Hindu.
Bangladesh (originally East Pakistan) was
created to accommodate Muslim Bengali in a
separate state. Bengali make up two thirds of
the population of Calcutta (see pages 76-93).

BHARIA *Population:* 94,000. Language:
Hindi (Indo-Aryan). This tribe, also known
as the Bharia-Bhumia, live in the forest and
hill region of the Satpura hills in Madhya
Pradesh. They have forgotten their original
tribal language as they have come into
increasing contact with nearby Hindu
villagers for whom they often work as farm

servants and field laborers. Their habits of
eating and dress have also changed. They cut
and sell forest firewood to neighboring
villagers. They also participate with their
neighbors in the worship of the local
Hindu deities.

BHIL *Population:* 1,683,000. Language
group: Indo-Aryan. The Bhil live widely
scattered in Gujarat, Rajasthan, Maharashtra
and Madhya Pradesh where they were once
semi-nomadic hunters and food-gatherers.
Some groups remain closely associated with
forest areas, but most now live settled in
villages where they grow dry crops such as
millet, maize, wheat, barley and pulses. Many
work as laborers and watchmen. Some sell
grass and firewood for cash. They have
adopted many of the Hindu beliefs and
practices of their neighbors, but remnants of
their tribal religion survive. They erect carved
stones and wooden posts as memorials to
their ancestors. Bhili is a distinct, unwritten,
tribal Aryan language.

BHOTIA *Population:* large but unspecified.
Language group: Tibeto-Burman. The
Bhotia, most of whom are physically
mongoloid, are a group of tribes who live
widely scattered high up along the Indo-
Tibetan and the Nepal-Tibet border in
Punjab, West Bengal, Arunachal Pradesh,
Bhutan, Sikkim and Nepal. 'Bhot' means

Tibet and many Bhotia represent an overflow from Tibet into the Himalayan border lands. In the districts of Almora and Garhwal the non-Tibetan border folk are also called Bhotia. The distinct groups of Bhotia have in common a tradition of trade between Tibet and the region in which they live. Until the Chinese rulers of Tibet restricted this trade the Bhotia lived semi-nomadic lives exchanging grain and other produce of the lower Himalayan regions for salt, wool and livestock in Tibetan markets.

BHUIYA *Population:* 574,000. Language: Munda. The Bhuiya live widespread in an area of southern Bihar and northern Orissa, frequently close to groups of Ho (q.v.) and Oraon (q.v.). They generally live 2-3,000 feet up in jungle-clad hills and high wooded valleys, although there are also Hinduized groups of Bhuiya who live in the plains below. They do some hunting but subsist on a vegetable diet of pumpkins, beans and yams – grown by slash-and-burn and using digging sticks in forest clearings – and edible roots and wild fruits. They have no plow-cattle. They periodically trade thatching grass, leaf plates, mustard seeds, baskets and firewood for rice with Hindu villagers. Each Bhuiya village is a settlement of ten to forty houses and a bachelors' house and has at its center, near the headman's house and the village goddess temple, a ritual pillar which they always take with them whenever they shift their village sites. Each village customarily has both a secular and a sacerdotal hereditary headman.

BHUMIJ *Population:* 309,000. Languages: Munda, Oriya and Bengali. The Bhumij live in southern Bihar and north-east Orissa. To the east they tend to speak their own Munda language while towards the west they have become increasingly Hinduized and speak only the language of the surrounding plains populations. Nowadays they are mainly settled farmers, though several sub-tribes specialize in occupations like oilpressing and preparing burnt lime. While they still present offerings and sacrifices through their own village priests they now employ Brahman to conduct their wedding and funerary rituals.

BHUTIA see BHOTIA

BIHARI *Population:* 56 million. Language: Bihari (Indo-Aryan). The Bihari, who live in the state of Bihar, share their region with 29 other tribes such as the Ho (q.v.) and the Santal (q.v.). Traditionally the Bihari are farmers growing rice, wheat, barley and some jute. Today, however, increasing numbers work in developing industries – principally coal mining. An extended free primary education means that many more young Bihari are literate and work in clerical and administrative jobs. The Bihari have a rich tradition of folk epics which have passed down through the generations by word of mouth. An ill-fated minority live in Bangladesh.

BIRHOR *Population:* 3,000. Language: Munda. The Birhor live on the edge of the Chota Nagpur plateau in Bihar and Madhya Pradesh. They are divided into two groups, one nomadic and the other sedentary. The deforestation of Chota Nagpur has forced many Birhor into contact with nearby Hindu villagers whose fields they work on or with whom they barter rope made from the bark of a forest creeper. The Birhor who live in forest settlements grow maize and beans by slash-and-burn agriculture. The nomadic Birhor wander in small groups of four to ten families and usually stay only a week or two at a time in an area of jungle before moving on. They are divided into exogamous clans with slightly varying ritual customs. The headman of a settlement is also its chief priest and propitiator of the spirits believed to cause illness.

BODO see KACHARI

BONDO *Population:* 5,000. Language: Munda. The Bondo are a small, distinctive tribe of the Eastern Ghats in southern Orissa. They call themselves Remo and speak a Munda dialect which has affinities with the Gadaba (q.v.) language. Bondo women wear nothing but a ten-inch wide waist cloth, which they spin and weave themselves, with a profusion of thick metal neckbands, brass chains and glass bead necklaces over their breasts and cloth headbands round their heads, which they customarily shave. The men wear loincloths with the odd bead necklace. They practise slash-and-burn cultivation, grow rice on irrigated plots, keep cattle, goats, pigs and chickens and consider rats a delicacy. They rarely hunt today, because of deforestation, but all the men of the village join in an annual ritual hunt. The women fish in hill streams and in stagnant rice-field water.

BURGHERS *Population:* 50,000. Language: English. The Burghers live in Sri Lanka and are the Eurasian descendants of the Dutch and other Europeans who served in the commercial and administrative services during the colonial period. Today's Burghers tend to be urban middle class. Many are clerks in commercial and government offices.

CHAKMA *Population:* 43,000. Language: Bengali (Indo-Aryan). The Chakma live in the valleys and plains of the Chittagong Hill tract in Bangladesh and in Tripura, Assam, and West Bengal. Most are slash-and-burn cultivators although some grow rice on the plains using a plow pulled by men or oxen. They grow maize, sesame and cotton. Like the Marma (q.v.) they were renowned for their craftsmanship in clay, iron, wood, and weaving but no longer practise any handicrafts. Most Chakma are Buddhists but have their own distinctive tribal rites.

CHENCHU *Population:* 18,000. Language: Telugu (Dravidian). The Chenchu are a primitive tribe who live in the forest areas of the Nallamalai Hills in Andhra Pradesh. They are racially Veddoid and physically and culturally resemble the Vedda (q.v.) of Sri Lanka. Their traditional style of life was semi-nomadic. Even today there is a minority of Chenchu groups who subsist mainly by collecting wild roots, tubers, berries, honey and edible leaves and, to a lesser extent, by hunting, living according to an archaic pattern which once must have prevailed throughout large areas of India. In the rainy season they live in conical huts. In the dry season they camp under flimsy shelters made of leafy branches, moving frequently with their few material possessions – bows and arrows, digging sticks, baskets and bits of cotton cloth – in pursuit of food in different parts of the forest. The Chenchu barter forest produce for iron implements, cloth and occasionally grain with the settled peasants on the plains. Some Chenchu now work as forest laborers for wages.

DAFLA *Population:* 16,000. Language group: Tibeto-Burman. The Dafla are a mongoloid tribe who inhabit an extensive hill-region of the Subansiri District of Arunachal Pradesh. They grow dry rice, millet and sweet potatoes by slash-and-burn on the hill-slopes. Some have taken up irrigated rice cultivation in imitation of their Apa Tani (q.v.) neighbors. They breed *bos frontalis* cattle and pigs and goats. Their settlements, which consist of a number of vast longhouses each inhabited by up to twelve families, are notable for having no overall village or tribal government. Their only social or political grouping is the longhouse group of families, an autonomous unit under the leadership of the senior male which co-operates only on a casual basis with the other households. Wealthy Dafla men marry many wives. Each wife has her own hearth and independently cultivates her crops. The women are skilled weavers. The Dafla are also potters and blacksmiths. They believe in many spirits which are propitiated with animal sacrifices.

DHELKI KHARIA see KHARIA

DIMASA see KACHARI

DOM see VALMIKI

DORLA see KOYA

DUDH KHARIA see KHARIA

DRAVIDIANS *Population:* 115 million. Language: Dravidian. Those people who speak Dravidian languages spread into India well before the Indo-Aryans. They were gradually pushed into south India where most of them now live. The major group is the Tamil (q.v.); Malayalam speakers of Kerala and Mysore are also Dravidian speakers. Their physical features vary from small, dark and negroid looking to isolated groups of tall Aryan looking peoples such as the Brahui of Baluchistan.

GADABA *Population:* 67,000. Language group: Munda. The Gadaba, who call themselves Guthan, live throughout a large region in the Eastern Ghats from south-east Madhya Pradesh through southern Orissa to north-east Andhra Pradesh. They are divided into hierarchically ranked sub-groups which do not intermarry and are subdivided into groups of families with a common surname. They grow millet and pulses by slash-and-burn, irrigated rice, and vegetables in plots behind their houses. Gadaba who have lost their lands to local money-lenders in the regions where the plains adjoin the hills work for wages as farm or road laborers.

Their houses are ranged in two parallel lines opening out onto a central village street, as in Jatapu (q.v.), Kond (q.v.) and Samantha (q.v.) villages. The roles of the traditional triumvirate of village leaders, the revenue collector headman, a man who ran ritual functions and their servant are now only informal since the government abolished the old system of revenue collection. Disputes are now arbitrated by a wealthy farmer or elder. The priest, who is also consulted on location of houses or auspicious marriage dates, presides over the marriage rituals and conducts the worship at the various festivals throughout the year, at which there is much ceremonial music and dancing.

GALLONG see ADI

GARO *Population:* 307,000. Language group: Tibeto-Burman. The Garo are, with the Khasi (q.v.), one of the two dominant tribes of the recently established hill state of Meghalaya. They are racially mongoloid and speak one of the Bodo group of languages. They grow rice, millet, maize and cotton by slash-and-burn on communally owned village lands. Their hill villages are of 150-200 houses. Their river-bank villages, in which their houses are built on piles, are smaller. Garo trace descent through the female line. Family property is inherited by daughters, not by sons. Women take the initiative in proposing marriage, and a new husband moves into his bride's house. Their children belong to the mother's clan. The Garo believe in a benevolent creator god and worship their ancestors represented by wood and stone figures. Today many are Christian converts, and hold ministerial posts in the government of Meghalaya.

GOND (pages 72-75)

GUJARATI *Population:* 27 million. Language group: Gujarati. The Gujarati are

Indo-Aryan people who live in the state of
Gujarat bordering Pakistan and the Indian
Ocean. Most of them earn a living from the
land. Cotton is their most important crop and
is made up into cloth in the local textile mills.
In Cutch they grow sorghum, sesamum and
pulses and – in the wetter east and south of the
region – maize and rice. Fifteen per cent of the
population live by industry, mainly mineral
production.

GUTHAN see GADABA

HO *Population:* 648,000. Language group:
Munda. The Ho are one of the largest
Munda-speaking tribes of Bihar and are
mainly concentrated in the Singbhum region,
although some 43,000 live in Orissa. 'Ho' is a
contraction of the word 'horo' which means
man. Until recently the Ho were largely
independent and there are still compact,
intact blocks of large Ho settlements of
substantial houses built of mud and roofed
with tiles. The Ho cultivate irrigated rice, as
well as millet, maize and other dry crops.
Their society is based on clans. Clan members
do not intermarry and descent is through the
male line. In every village there is one clan
with dominant traditional rights to the land,
and its own council.

IRULAR *Population:* 91,000. Language
group: Dravidian. Irular, or Irulan, is a
blanket term for a number of racially Veddoid
tribes who live in the forests of the Nilgiris,
the Palghat district of Kerala, and North
Arcot. Originally semi-nomadic hunters and
food-gatherers who subsisted on the wild
products of the forests, many now work as
forest laborers and collect forest produce for
sale. Most now cultivate either permanent
fields or, more often, hillsides by slash-and-
burn. The digging-over and planting of a
hillside is a communal affair done to the
sound of drums. The Irular live in temporary
houses built of wood and bamboo in small
settlements. They bury their dead in a sitting
posture.

JAINS *Population:* 1.5 million. Language
group: Hindi. The Jains are a religious group
living mainly in western India, in Gujarat.
The founder of Jainism was Mahavira
(c599-527 BC), an aristocrat of the warrior

caste. Jainism is based on non-violence and
ascetism.

JAT see SIKH

JATAPU *Population:* 74,000. Language
group: Dravidian. The Jatapu live in the hills
of north-eastern Andhra Pradesh and
adjacent areas of Orissa. Most grow maize,
pulses and millets by shifting cultivation,
chilies, tobacco and vegetables in backyard
plots. The tribes are divided into clans whose
members do not intermarry, each made up of
a number of family groups with a common
surname. Each Jatapu village, of two parallel
lines of continuous long-houses, has a
headman whose assistant organizes and
conducts festivals and ceremonies. In some
villages Brahman are employed to perform
rituals which were once the tribal priest's
prerogative. The tribal priest remains
prominent in the worship of the tribal deity,
Jakara Devta, who must be propitiated with
sacrifices of pigs, sheep or water buffalo.
Transvestite shamans ascertain the causes and
cures for personal misfortune and illness.

JUANG *Population:* 2,000. Language group:
Munda. The Juang live in the hills north-west
of Cuttack in northern Orissa. Juang men
dress in loincloths and women wear only
brief skirts and necklaces. They are an
agricultural tribe who cultivate millet, pulses
and oilseed by the slash-and-burn method
and grow rice on wet lands near stream beds.
All their land is communally owned and
cultivated. Each village has its hereditary
secular headman, his assistant, a hereditary
priest or religious head, and a shaman who
deals with disease-causing spirits. The hub of
the village community is the *majang* or men's
house which serves as a courthouse for the
village council. It is also the dormitory for
unmarried males over seven. After initiation
when they are 15 the boys join a youth
organization arranged in a series of
hierarchically ranked age-groups each with
different status, rights and obligations. The
young married man who is its elected leader is
the intermediary between the youth
organization and the village headman and
council. Dancing and singing feature
prominently in village life. Boys frequently go
on dancing exhibitions to other villages to
meet prospective brides.

KACHARI *Population:* 236,000. Language
group: Tibeto-Burman. The Kachari are one
of the most numerous and important
populations of Assam. As early as the 13th
century a great Kachari kingdom extended
along the south bank of the Brahmaputra
from the Dikhu river as far as the Kallang,
and included the Dhansiri valley. In the
Brahmaputra valley the Kachari now call
themselves Bodo, and in the North Cachar
hills they call themselves Dimasa. They live
among the low hills. Those who live in the
plains have adopted Hinduism outwardly,
and live like other Hindus but also maintain
their own system of beliefs by a system of
syncretism. The houses of a village stand in
two rows facing one another with the men's
house or bachelors' dormitory in the center.

KADAR *Population:* 1,250. Language group:
Dravidian. The Kadar are a small and very
primitive forest tribe of Kerala. Until
recently they were semi-nomadic hunters and
food gatherers, subsisting entirely on wild
forest produce. Their main implements were
bow and arrow, and the digging stick. Today
some Kadar have settled down as cultivators,
but the majority collect forest produce for
barter or sale, help in elephant capturing
operations or work for the forest department.
Their religion is an amalgam of old tribal
beliefs and Hindu practices.

KAGWARIA see KOL

KANIKAR *Population:* 11,000. Language group: Dravidian. The Kanikar, also known as Kani, are a jungle tribe who inhabit the mountains of south Travancore. Some Kanikar have settled close to towns. Those who live in the hills have no permanent abode but move from one part of the forest to another in search of new land for slash-and-burn cultivation. Their huts made of bamboo are so flimsy that they can easily be erected wherever cultivable land is available. Today the Kanikar are also employed by government agencies to collect forest produce and trap elephants. They speak a Malayalam dialect with a strong Tamil influence. In their religious practices rituals connected with clearing land and the growth of crops are of special importance, but the worship of Hindu deities is gradually gaining ground.

KASHMIRI (pages 98–105)

KATHODIA see KATKARI

KATKARI *Population:* 143,000. Language group: Indo-Aryan. The Katkari tribe, or Kathodia, are scattered over a large area of the Western Ghats including the Thana and Kolaba districts of Maharashtra and some parts of Gujarat. They are related to the Bhil (q.v.), and like the Bhil have a traditional association with life in the forest. Even in areas between Bombay and Poona as late as the 1950s there were groups of Katkari who led a semi-nomadic existence as hunters and food-gatherers who used the bow and arrow and the digging-stick as their principal implements. Other groups too were traditionally engaged in the collection and sale of various forest produce, such as charcoal, but many Katkari have settled down as ordinary cultivators or agricultural laborers.

KAWAR *Population:* 334,000. Language: Hindi. The Kawar live in the hilly area of Chattisgarh in Madhya Pradesh. They are thought by their neighbors to be hardly distinguishable from the Gond (q.v.) though there is no connection between them.

KHAIRWAR *Population:* 155,000. Language group: Dravidian. The Khairwar live on the Chota Nagpur plateau in Bihar and Madhya Pradesh. They are divided into groups frequently named after plants or animals. Their religious practices are basically Hindu.

KHARIA *Population:* 225,000. Language group: Munda. The Kharia are divided into three groups spread between Orissa, Madhya Pradesh and Bihar. Each division, none of which intermarries with the other, represents a different level of technology. The Pahari Kharia of Orissa who live isolated in forested hills are mainly food gatherers, hunters, and shifting cultivators. The Dhelki Kharia of Madhya Pradesh practise settled agriculture and have a more complex social and religious system, but stand on a lower level of material culture than the Dudh Kharia of Bihar.

KHASI *Population:* 364,000. Language group: Mon-Khmer. The Khasi, a mongoloid people who speak dialects related to the Mon language of Burma and the Khmer language of Cambodia, are the dominant community in the recently constituted state of Meghalaya. Many are highly educated and fill political and executive positions in the state. Material modernization and widespread conversion to Christianity have only marginally affected traditional Khasi family life. All family property is inherited by the youngest daughter who holds it in trust for the family, and who performs all religious ceremonies. On marriage a man moves into his wife's house. If his wife is not a youngest daughter he may later set up a separate household with his wife and children, provided he has shown himself able to support them. Traditionally there are four Khasi classes: the royal clan, the priestly clan, the ministerial clan and the plebeian clan.

KOL *Population:* 432,000. Languages: Hindi, Marathi, Oriya (Indo-Aryan). The Kol are scattered from central Madhya Pradesh south into Maharashtra and south-east into Orissa. They comprise several sub-tribes such as the Routela, Rautia, Thakuria and Kagwaria. They have abandoned their tribal language and now speak the languages of the village populations.

KOLAM *Population:* 60,000. Languages: Kolami (Dravidian) and Marathi (Indo-Aryan). The Kolam live in the northernmost part of Andhra Pradesh, where they speak their own tribal tongue, Kolami, as well as Telugu, and in adjacent regions of Maharashtra, where they speak Marathi.

139

They frequently live near the Gond (q.v.) with whom they share many cultural features. Traditionally shifting cultivators, rapid deforestation and government prohibition of shifting cultivation has brought them into increasing contact with the plainspeople. Kolam tribespeople's staple foods are maize, pulses and, most important, *jowar*, a coarse millet which they eat in a form of gruel. They now grow these by settled agriculture using plows and bullocks. High costs of cattle and maintenance have forced Kolam to be increasingly indebted to moneylenders.

Kolam settlements are of small, unaligned, rectangular houses. The Kolam are divided into 'brother clans' with whom they may not marry, and 'in-law clans' with whom they may. A settlement is led by a headman who presides over disputes and councils concerned with village welfare. There is also a village priest who performs marriages and leads in the worship of their deities. Kolam festivals resemble Gond (q.v.) festivals, but Kolam differ from Gond in having no separate clan-deities or ritual bards. Each clan in the village has its own special dance drum. On some occasions, while the women dance in a circle, ritual clowns—dressed in high peacock feather headdresses and adorned with body paint, bells and false beards – circulate, mimicking them.

KOND *Population:* 846,000. Language group: Dravidian. The Kond are a tribal group concentrated mainly in Orissa that extends into Andhra Pradesh and Madhya Pradesh. 512,000 speak their original tribal language, Kui, while others have adopted

Oriya and other regional languages. Traditionally shifting cultivators who used axe and hoe as their main implements, but now prohibited from this practice by the government, many Kond now cultivate rice on irrigated fields. Most Kond tribespeople live in separate villages usually of two lines of houses facing each other. Even where they live in mixed villages Kond live in separate streets. In the 19th century the Kond attained considerable notoriety when British officials mounted a campaign for the suppression of human sacrifice, known as Meriah sacrifice, which the Kond performed to improve the fertility of their crops. Later buffalo were substituted for the human victims. The forked wooden pillars to which the buffalo are tied for the triennial sacrifice are left standing at the four stones which represent the Shrine of the Earth Goddess in the middle of the village.

KONDA DORA *Population:* 12,000. Language group: Dravidian. The Konda Dora, also known as Konda Kapu, live in the forested hill tracts of the Eastern Ghats in north-east Andhra Pradesh and Orissa. They are slash-and-burn farmers and cultivate millet, beans and oilseeds but supplement their diet in the lean season by digging up edible roots. Each village, a settlement of 20 to 40 houses, has a headman responsible to outside revenue collectors, an internal tribal leader, a traditional priest and numerous village elders who are occasionally called to arbitrate disputes and conflicts. The Konda Dora are organized in clans whose members may not intermarry. Descent is through the father's line. All a man's sons and their families usually live together as a joint family. The Konda Dora stand in a caste-like hierarchical relation to neighboring tribes.

KONDA KAPU see KONDA DORA

KONYAK (see NAGA pages 106-109)

KORKU *Population:* 185,000. Language group: Munda. This tribe, whose name in their own language means 'men' or 'tribesmen', inhabit a wide area of central India in the Satpura and Madadeo hills of Madhya Pradesh over to the Chota Nagpur plateau of Bihar. Their women wear their sari to calf-length and draw the sari-end over their heads into a hood, with a large nose-ring

in their left nostril and many bead necklaces, bangles, and metal anklets. This tribe formerly lived by hunting and shifting cultivation in the forests and in some areas Korku were notorious as robbers. They are now more dependent upon sedentary agriculture growing millet and keeping pigs and chickens, and only occasionally hunting and fishing. From the mohuwa flower they distil an intoxicating drink. Their villages are of about twenty mud huts with roofs thatched with grass placed over a layer of leaves. They are divided into four territorially based and hierarchically ranked sub-groups, within which are clans which have names of plants or animals. Marriage between members of the same clan is forbidden. Their principal deities are the sun and the moon.

Their everyday life is more frequently influenced by their village deities: Dongar Deo – god of the hills, Mutua Deo – a god of the village and curer of sickness, and Mata – the smallpox goddess. The rituals to these deities are performed by the village priest, who also performs the Korku wedding rituals and is frequently employed by neighboring Hindu villagers to perform the worship of their village deities.

KORWA *Population:* 67,000. Language group: Munda. The Korwa are a tribe who live chiefly in the easternmost districts of Madhya Pradesh. Some also live in the Satpura and Mahadeo hills of Madhya Pradesh and are akin to the Korku (q.v.). They were hunters and gatherers and some practised rudimentary agriculture until deforestation and expanding plains populations forced increased contact with the outside world. They are now frequently employed in trading forest produce or as farm laborers.

KOTA *Population:* 956. Language group: Dravidian. The Kota are a small community of artisans and musicians who live in seven villages in the Nilgiris hills of Madras state. A relationship of mutual dependence links them economically and ritually with the pastoral Toda (q.v.) and the agricultural Badaga (q.v.) to whom they are socially inferior. As well as cultivating crops there are among them expert blacksmiths, goldsmiths, silversmiths, carpenters, potters and tanners. At the funerals and other rituals of Toda and Badaga they act as musicians. The Kota observe two funeral ceremonies: the 'green funeral' soon after a death, when the body is cremated: and the annual or bi-annual 'dry funeral' for all who died since the last funeral. In each village there is a large square ground, walled in with stones with, at its center, two thatched shrines dedicated to a divine couple.

KOYA *Population:* 140,000. Language group: Dravidian. The Koya, or Dorla, are a sub-tribe of the Gond (q.v.) and inhabit the parts of Madhya Pradesh and Andhra Pradesh on both sides of the lower course of the Godavari river. Some still speak a Gondi dialect, but most of those in Andhra Pradesh now speak Telugu. The loss of their original language has been accompanied by an impoverishment of their mythology and religious ideas, and the dividing line between the tribal religion and the Hinduism of the local Telugu peasantry is being blurred. Moreover, the large-scale influx of Hindu castes has deprived the Koya of much of their ancestral land and many Koya are now industrial laborers.

KUKI *Population:* 29,000. Language group: Tibeto-Burman, The Kuki are a group of mongoloid tribes scattered over the Chittagong hill tracts, Tripura, North Cachar hills and Nagaland. Many have moved from Burma into India in search of cultivable land. Within India there have been similar migrations caused by the Kuki's traditional system of slash-and-burn cultivation. The Kuki have an institution of village headmen whose position is tied to one particular clan. There is a system of inheritance according to which only the oldest and the youngest son inherit, while the middle sons have no right to the paternal property. The Kuki worship their tribal gods with sacrifices of goats and fowl.

KUTTIA KOND see KOND

KUVI see SAMANTHA

LACCADIVE ISLANDERS *Population:* 25,000. Languages: Malayalam, Sinhalese. The people of these Arabian Sea islands off the south-west coast of India are of mixed Hindu and Arab descent. Peoples of many of these atolls still remember their Hindu ancestry and tell legends about their conversion to Islam by an Arab saint. Their diet consists mainly of fish, vegetables, bananas and coconuts. They use fiber from the coconut husk to make ropes and matting. These and other produce they trade with the mainland people for rice which is not grown on the islands.

LAMBADA *Population:* 118,000. Language group: Indo-Aryan. The Lambada, also known as Banjara or Sukali, are a formerly nomadic population concentrated in Andhra Pradesh and Mysore, but also living scattered in Madhya Pradesh, Orissa and Delhi. Their traditional home was Rajasthan where, particularly during the Mogul Empire, they used to be wandering traders and carriers who transported goods with their caravans of pack-bullocks between Rajputana, Central India and the Deccan. They still trade in grain, salt and turmeric in areas where pack animals have an advantage over wheeled traffic and barter with Gond (q.v.), Bhil (q.v.) and other forest tribes. They also breed cattle and make an income by selling dairy produce. They tend to retain their tribal culture and language even where they have settled as sedentary farmers. Lambada women are easily recognizable by their colorful, lavishly embroidered clothes and their great quantities of heavy ornaments.

LEPCHA *Population:* 30,000. Language group: Tibeto-Burman. The Lepcha are a mongoloid group who inhabit parts of Sikkim, western Bhutan and west Bengal. In Sikkim and in the adjoining areas of India to Darjeeling district, where Bhotia (q.v.) and Nepali are later immigrants, they represent the indigenous population. Before the establishment of Bhotia rule there were only local chiefs among the Lepcha. The Lepcha practise both shifting and irrigated types of cultivation and keep cattle, goats and pigs.

When the Bhotia emigrated from Tibet the pagan Lepcha were largely converted to Buddhism. The village temple became the focal point for their integration into the Buddhist culture of the Bhotia rulers, but many of the old ritual practices survived. Indigenous belief and Tibetan Buddhism were closely interwoven, to produce one of the distinctive cultures of the Himalayan region. Lepcha still, contrary to Buddhist doctrine, perform animal sacrifices. Killing a cow or goat is part of their funeral rites. They practise a form of polyandry by which a married woman is expected to have sexual relations with her husband's brothers and certain other kinsmen. Moreover a Lepcha can inherit the wife of any elder brother as well as the wife of an uncle.

LUSHAI see MIZO

MAHARASHTRI *Population:* 50 million. Language: Marathi. The Maharashtri live in the state of Maharashtra formed in 1960 when Bombay state was divided into this Marathi-speaking state and Gujarat. Nearly two-thirds of the Maharashtri are farmers. Rice and wheat are the main crops but they also grow cash crops such as cotton for local textile industries, tobacco, sugar and groundnuts. Nearly 30 per cent of the population live in towns. Maharashtra is one of the most industrialized states of India and Maharashtri work in factories producing cars, bicycles, light metal goods, matches and chemicals. Many Maharashtri are well educated: the state has a high literacy rate. They are mostly Hindus but there are some Jains (q.v.).

MALDIVE ISLANDERS *Population:* 98,000. Language group: Indo-Aryan. The people of the independent Sultanate of the Maldives inhabit 220 islands of the total 2,000 which form the atoll. They have maintained constant contacts and trade with nearby Sri Lanka (Ceylon), and are racially and linguistically south Asian. Their geographical position on a traditional Arab trade route, however, has led to their conversion to Islam. They cultivate millet, coconuts and tropical fruits, but their main industry is fishing.

MARMA *Population:* 95,000. Language: Arakanese (a dialect of Burmese, Tibeto-Burman). The Marma, or Magh, live in the valleys and plains of the Mong and Bomong regions of the Chittagong hill tracts in Bangladesh. They probably came originally from the Arakan hills driven out by Burmese invaders in the 18th century. Their men wear skirt-like sarongs which the older men supplement with a small white cloth wrapped as a turban. Marma women wear Burmese-style sarongs fastened at the waist with a tailored blouse. They are slash-and-burn farmers who grow maize, sesame, cotton and

141

rice. They also specialize in bamboo work and use bamboo to construct their houses which are generally built on six-feet stilts. They are Buddhists but concentrate on propitiating malevolent and evil spirits.

MIKIR *Population:* 155,000. Language group: Tibeto-Burman. The Mikir are a mongoloid people concentrated in the Mikir Hills in Assam with smaller communities in the Jaintia Hills. They build their houses on piles close to their fields, and when the cultivated land is exhausted they move the settlement to wherever new land is available for cultivation. The villages consist of only a small number of houses, each of which contains several closely related families. The heads of the individual households form a council which manages village affairs. They believe in a plurality of deities and spirits, the most powerful of whom is the god of heaven.

MINYONG (see ADI)

MIZO *Population:* 222,000. Language group: Tibeto-Burman. The term Mizo is the new name for a group of tribes previously known as Lushai, whose homeland was recently constituted as the Union Territory of Mizoram. With some allied tribes they are believed to have migrated from the upper basins of the Irrawaddy and Chindwin rivers of Upper Burma, and settled in the 17th century in their present habitat. Slash-and-burn cultivation is the traditional basis of their economy, and it is closely linked with the tribe's migratory habits. Powerful hereditary chiefs used to exert almost unlimited authority over their subjects. Today most Mizo lead a more settled life. Many abandoned their old tribal religion and have adopted Christianity. As a result of the work of missionaries their educational progress has been spectacular. Modern political activities led to the creation of the autonomous region of Mizoram.

MUNDA *Population:* 999,000. Language group: Munda (Austro-Asiatic). The Munda, who have given their name to the entire western branch of the Austro-Asiatic language, are one of the most populous of the

aboriginal tribes who speak languages of that group. Their physical type evinces strong Veddoid (Vedda q.v.) elements, and they have a very dark skin color. Their greatest concentration is in Bihar, where they live in compact blocks on the Chota Nagpur plateau, but there are also Munda in Orissa and in west Bengal. Their large villages, of solid houses built of timber, bamboo and mud, are grouped in clusters, in each of which the members of one specific clan predominate. They cultivate rice, millet, maize and cotton with plows and bullocks. They rarely harness bullocks to carts, but transport all goods on their shoulders and heads. The most notable feature of a Munda village is its burial ground where stone pillars and slabs covering graves commemorate the dead. These megalithic monuments, some of which seem to stem from prehistoric epochs, are still being erected. About half the Munda have been converted to Christianity, and in many villages Christians and adherents of the old tribal religion live side by side.

MURIA see GOND

NAGA (pages 106-109)

NIKOBARESE *Population:* 15,000. Language group: Mon Khmer. The Nikobarese live on the Nikobar Islands, an archipelago which extends north-west from Sumatra, but belongs politically to India. The Nikobarese are racially distinct from the adjacent Indonesians and Andamanese, but their Mon-Khmer language suggests ancient associations with the south-east Asian mainland. Their traditional dwellings are built on stilts in village clusters of ten to twelve huts. Leadership is provided by a non-hereditary village headman and a council of elders. There is no inheritance of land, although coconut trees, huts, and canoes are inherited. For food they rely heavily on the coconut and a bread-like paste preparation made from cooked pandanus seeds. They fish, and save their pigs and chickens for festivals. They are fond of toddy, the sap of the palm tree which they tap to make an intoxicating drink. Coconuts are the islanders' chief export.

ORAON *Population:* 1,142,000. Language group: Dravidian. The Oraon are the second largest Dravidian-speaking tribal group of India and inhabit the Chota Nagpur plateau of Bihar, as well as large areas in Orissa, Bengal and Madhya Pradesh. They have always been mainly an agricultural community growing millet, pulses and oil-seeds, and rice on low-lying irrigated fields. They also rear cattle, fish and hunt. The young men of a bachelors' dormitory sometimes work together as a labor-group. Although farm land is traditionally owned by the clan the actual unit of agricultural production is the joint family headed by the senior man. All sons inherit land, but the eldest gets a small plot in excess of his normal share. Today many Oraon have been converted to Christianity. Some Oraon have now been drawn into industrial employment and live in such towns as Ranchi.

PUNJABI *Population:* 17 million. Language: Punjabi. The Punjabi live in Pakistan and the Indian state of Punjab which was re-formed to accommodate the Sikhs in Harijana in 1966. The history of the Punjabi has been influenced by the four frontier passes that connect Afghanistan to the Punjabi plains. Aryan-speaking people first migrated through these passes early in the second millennium BC. The infiltration was slow and gradual and probably extended over centuries. The Indo-Aryan race first entered the Punjab about 1500 BC. Muslim invaders conquered the region around 1000 AD. Most Punjabi are Muslim or Sikh (q.v.). They are a virile people, with a talent as fighters. They grow wheat, cotton and millet on irrigated land.

RAUTIA see KOL

ROUTELA see KOL

PAIDI see VALMIKI

PAIKARA see KAWAR

PARDHAUS see GOND

PARSEES (pages 54-57)

RAJASTHANI *Population:* 26 million. Language group: Hindi. The Rajasthani are of Indo-Aryan stock. They live in Rajasthan in the north-west of India bordering Pakistan. Rainfall is scant and in the irrigated areas wheat, barley, cotton and groundnuts are grown. The Rajasthani also grow millets, sesamum and pulses. Sheep and goats are kept throughout the country, except in the Thar desert, and camels are used for transport. The Rajasthani produce 90 per cent of India's gypsum mainly for the Sindri fertilizer factory in Bihar. They also produce limestone, mica, lead, zinc, steatite, iron ore and emeralds.

REDDI *Population:* 35,000. Language group: Telugu. Reddi, the name of a large land-holding Hindu caste of Andhra Pradesh, is also applied to an aboriginal tribe known as Hill or Konda Reddi. They live in the hills to both sides of the Godavari where the river breaks through the Eastern Ghats, and are a typical example of the primitive shifting cultivators of the Deccan. Traditional settlements are of three or four square houses, built of timber and bamboo, set in the depth of the forest, close to a hill-side where the forest has been cleared and crops of millet and maize are grown. Many Reddi have now moved down from the hills and settled in larger villages on the bank of the Godavari.

The Reddi tribal religion centers mainly on the cult of deities of hills and forests, who are propitiated with blood sacrifices, and the worship of Mother Earth. In the past certain deities had to be appeased with human sacrifices.

SAMANTHA *Population:* 5,400. Language group: Dravidian. The Samantha, or Kuvi, live about 2,500 feet up in the forest tracts of the Eastern Ghats in north-east Andhra Pradesh. They share many ethnic characteristics with the Kond (q.v.). Their men wear a loin-cloth and keep their long hair tied up in a bun at the back of their heads. Samantha women tie their sari in a way distinct from the plainswomen with a separate wide tubular cloth draped and secured at one shoulder. They grow millet, maize, chilies and castor by shifting cultivation and supplement their diet with vegetables and edible tubers and roots which they gather in the forest. They trade leaf plates for the plains villagers to use as disposable plates for large feasts and in restaurants in the towns.

SANTAL *Population:* 3,247,000. Language group: Munda. The Santal are the largest of the Munda-speaking tribes occupying compact areas in Bihar, Orissa and west Bengal. The Santal were formerly a forest-tribe engaged in shifting cultivation, food-gathering, hunting and fishing. By extracting oil from the wild seeds and manufacturing lime they provided themselves with products which could be used for barter with economically more advanced populations. At present they cultivate with plows and bullocks, but largely as share-croppers and agricultural laborers. Every Santal village has its own headman and priest. The Santal now enjoy hunts as occasions for a tribal reunion, although there is little game. There is a hunt-council at which matters of common interest are discussed, disputes are settled, and there is dancing, singing and drinking.

SAORA *Population:* 256,000. Language group: Munda. The Saora are a tribe who live widely scattered over large areas of Orissa, Madhya Pradesh, and Andhra Pradesh. As some groups have been assimilated into local Hindu populations, adopting their language, dress, manners and gods, the Saora may total 400,000. In ancient Indian literature Saora

are described as wild, martial people. Traditional Saora culture has been preserved mainly in the hills of Orissa where they grow tobacco, maize, ginger and rice. Their villages are of long rows of houses built wall to wall and linked by a common veranda. Their society is based on the extended family descended from a male ancestor. It is also divided into a chiefly class and commoners who do not intermarry although chiefs may occasionally marry commoner girls. Saora shamans establish contact with the world of spirits and gods in a state of trance and enter formal marriages with spirit-spouses.

SAURIA PAHARIA *Population:* 56,000. Language group: Dravidian. The Sauria Paharia inhabit the hills of the Santal Parganas in east central Bihar. Their women dress distinctively in a short skirt-like sari and no blouse. They practise shifting cultivation and rely mainly on digging sticks rather than plows to raise their staple crop, maize, but hunt and gather forest produce less than formerly. They rear pigs, cattle and chickens. Their villages, of rows of wattled bamboo grass-thatched houses, are on level ground high on the hills. Before marriage the husband usually goes to live and work for his prospective bride's family for an agreed period before the wedding. Each village has its council of elders presided over by a headman. Leaders in the ritual sphere are the village priest and his assistant—who perform animal sacrifices presided over by the priest.

SIKH (pages 94-97)

SINDHI *Population:* 7,630,000. Language: Sindhi. The Sindhi live in the lower Indus valley and delta in Pakistan. Their climate is dry and hot for most of the year and crops can only be grown with the aid of canal irrigation from the Indus. Rice is the main crop but cotton, wheat, pulses, oilseeds, barley and vegetables are grown in different parts as well. Most Sindhi are Muslim.

SINHALESE *Population:* 7 million. Language group: Sinhalese. The Sinhalese are the majority ethnic group of Sri Lanka (Ceylon) who inhabit all but the northernmost part of the island. Their language has affinities with North Indian languages. The

Sinhalese distinguish between the up-country people *(uda rata minissu)* and the low-country people *(pahata rata minissu)*. The former are the inhabitants of the central hill region of the island which formed the Kandyan Kingdom, which remained independent until 1815. Their manner of speech and vocabulary distinguish them from the other group who inhabit the coastal plains, who were under extensive European influence from 1505. Until recently the up-country people tended to feel superior and refrained from intermarriage with the low-country people.

Socially and culturally the Sinhalese have much in common with neighboring India. While Buddhism has died out in India, however, it has remained strong and flourished among the Sinhalese. **(pages 114-127)**

TAMIL OF SOUTH INDIA (pages 110-113)

TAMIL OF SRI LANKA *Population:* 2,400,000. Language: Tamil. Tamil living in Sri Lanka are divided into two groups: the descendants of Tamil-speaking immigrants from south India who started settling in the north of the island before the 2nd century AD and the descendants of Tamil laborers brought by the British from India to work on the tea, coffee and rubber plantations from the mid-19th century. The former live around the northern town of Jaffna and the north-east coast. The latter live in the central hill region where most of the plantations are. The Tamil have a long history of competition and conflict with the Sinhalese (q.v.). Sinhalese are Buddhists while the Tamil are Hindus.

TODA *Population:* 714. Language group: Dravidian. The Toda are a small pastoral tribe in the Nilgiris hills, whose prominence in anthropological literature is disproportionate to their number. The Toda represent a classic example of pastoral life centered on the buffalo. They traditionally exchange dairy products and occasionally meat and buffalo calves with their neighbors for all that they require. The Badaga (q.v.) provide them with grain and other farm-products, and also act as middlemen between the Toda and traders from the lowlands. The Kota (q.v.) supply them with pottery and ironware.

The Toda have an unusual marriage and kinship system. The tribe is divided into two

sections within which marriages are made, each of which is divided into a number of clans who may not intermarry. Promiscuity is institutionalized: every male of one clan has a claim over every woman of certain other clans. As paternity is often uncertain, some months before a child's birth its legal father is chosen by common consent. Certain Toda buffalo are sacred, and the dairy in which their milk is churned is for all intents and purposes the temple of the tribe. The churning is carried out ritualistically by priests to the accompaniment of prescribed prayers.

VALMIKI *Population:* 22,354. Language: Telugu (Dravidian). The Valmiki, also called Dom or Paidi, inhabit the forests of the Eastern Ghats in north-east Andhra Pradesh and are frequently identified with certain Harijan. Their close connection with the plains is attested to by their plains-style dress, their exclusive use of the plains language, and their traditional occupation as traders and middlemen between tribal and plains markets. They live on hill slopes in settlements which they sometimes share with the Bagata (q.v.), who consider them as untouchables and live in a separate section of the settlement. By adopting Hinduized customs the Valmiki have recently challenged the dominance of the numerically smaller Bagata, who force them to use separate wells or water sources and to show customary signs of deference. The Valmiki are divided into two subgroups who eat with each other but do not intermarry. Each settlement has a council of five elders, presided over by a headman and his assistant, which plays a prominent role at marriages, funerals and festivals. They consult a shaman on auspicious times for ceremonies.

VEDDA (pages 128-129)

WARLI *Population:* 374,000. Language group: Indo-Aryan. The Warli tribe inhabit some of the forest areas of Maharashtra and Gujarat. Like the Bhil (q.v.) originally a semi-nomadic jungle tribe subsisting mainly on game and the collection of wild produce, they have now become largely settled cultivators. They still use the digging stick to gather wild roots. They collect grass and firewood for sale. They worship a number of tribal deities offering them grain and

sacrificing animals, although they are now influenced by Hinduism.

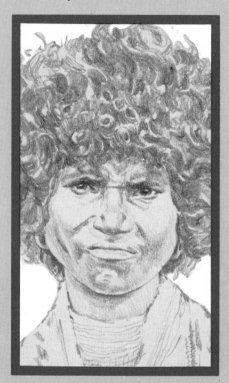

YANADI *Population:* 205,000. Language: Telugu. The Yanadi are scattered over southern coastal Andhra Pradesh but concentrated in the area of Pulicat lake. They live in small clusters of conical huts, six feet in diameter, made of palmyra palm leaves fastened to a bamboo frame. Traditionally a gypsy-like nomadic group they now tend to settle semi-permanently on the outskirts of Hindu villages. Despite government efforts to turn them into cultivators they still fish with nets and conical fish traps along the coast, hunt small game and gather honey in the interior forested areas. Or they work for villagers as farm laborers or take jobs as watchmen and construction workers.

The Yanadi are subdivided into Reddi, Yanadi, Adavi Yanadi, Kappala Yanadi, Challa Yanadi. Members of superior subgroups refuse to intermarry or eat with members of inferior groups. They are notable for their lack of leaders such as headmen or clan heads, although these may have existed in the past. Serious cases are adjudicated by *ad hoc* councils of respected tribal elders. Their tribal patron deity is said to be Chenchu Devara, which suggests an ancient connection with the Chenchu tribe (q.v.).

All population figures are approximate